S0-ARM-474

Signatures

Skills Assessment Reading and Language Arts

TEACHER'S EDITION

GRADE

5

Senior Author

Roger C. Farr

HARCOURT BRACE

Copyright © by Harcourt Brace & Company

All rights reserved. No part of this publication may be reproduced or transmitted in any form or by any means, electronic or mechanical, including photocopy, recording, or any information storage and retrieval system.

Teachers using SIGNATURES may photocopy complete pages in sufficient quantities for classroom use only and not for resale.

HARCOURT BRACE and Quill Design is a registered trademark of Harcourt Brace & Company.

Printed in the United States of America

ISBN 0-15-307795-6

1 2 3 4 5 6 7 8 9 10 085 99 98 97 96

Table of Contents

APPENDIX

Coping Masters

Theme 1
Skills Assessment: Reading
Skills Assessment: Language Arts

Theme 2
Skills Assessment: Reading
Skills Assessment: Language Arts

Theme 3
Skills Assessment: Reading
Skills Assessment: Language Arts

Theme 4
Skills Assessment: Reading
Skills Assessment: Language Arts

Theme 5
Skills Assessment: Reading
Skills Assessment: Language Arts

Theme 6
Skills Assessment: Reading
Skills Assessment: Language Arts

Harcourt Brace School Publishers • Skills Assessment

ASSESSMENT AND EVALUATION IN *SIGNATURES*

by Roger C. Farr

Assessment gets much attention these days. There is no lessening of the plea for accountability. A wide range of informal and formal assessments is being touted as the solution to classroom assessment. We hear a great deal about authentic assessments, portfolio assessments, performance assessments, kid watching, running records, anecdotal records, and holistic assessments, to name just some of the terms being used.

Every good assessment program should be more than a willy-nilly collection of tests, observations, and checklists. An assessment program should be integral to instruction. The Harcourt Brace assessments have been carefully designed to provide teachers and schools with the information they need at the time they need that information. The Harcourt Brace assessments provide a comprehensive picture of students' achievements as they progress through the program. That picture will provide the basis for school and classroom planning.

Thinking about assessment as an attempt to get a picture of what students are learning and are able to do provides a useful analogy. When a teacher or school gets a valid look at where students are and what they are able to do, they can plan what they need to do to complete the picture. If we think of assessment as a picture on an easel, we can consider the three main components of assessment that hold up that easel. These three legs delineate the three main purposes for assessment: 1) finding out what students know; 2) determining if they can apply what they know; and 3) learning about students' abilities to self-assess.

The first leg of the assessment easel is to find out what students know. There is no question that students need to know skills and strategies, to comprehend literal meanings, and to recognize letters and words. There is a place for knowing, and good assessment provides information about what students know. Short-answer and multiple-choice assessments can provide useful information about what students know. Teacher observation, student work samples, and teacher/student discussions are also valuable sources of information about what students know.

The second leg of assessment is to determine if students can apply what they know. Knowing by itself is not enough. Students have to apply what they know. Finding out if students can apply what they know is the second leg of the assessment easel. Good readers and writers solve problems, read between the lines, and create their own stories and interpretations of what they read. Performance assessments, holistic writing activities, and

Harcourt Brace School Publishers • Skills Assessment

classroom portfolios are crucial if teachers are to find out whether students can go beyond just knowing to applying. Good performance assessments and activities should be integrated with instruction and should provide realistic activities that engage a student's mind.

The third leg of assessment is to engage students in self-assessment. If students are to continue to learn, they must be able to self-assess. They have to review their ideas, their projects, and their writing and learn how to improve what they are doing. Those who are successful in the world are those who learn how to figure out a way to do it better. This third leg of assessment combines instruction and assessment. As you help students to self-assess, they begin to self-assess. You watch them progress as self-assessors. They apply what they learn to become more effective readers and writers. Portfolio conferences, teacher/student discussions of work samples, and similar activities are all part of helping students become more effective self-assessors.

These three legs of the assessment easel were the basis for planning the Harcourt Brace assessments. You may want to examine the assessments in *Signatures* with this outline in mind. *Which of the assessments help to determine what students know? Which of the assessments focus on the application of what students know? Which of the assessments help students to become more effective self-assessors?*

Listed below is a brief overview of the assessment tools available in *Signatures*.

Integrated Performance Assessment
Six Integrated Performance Assessments correlated to themes in the student anthologies are available at each level of the program. These reading-writing tasks give students opportunities to construct personal interpretations of authentic literature and to apply their writing skills in meaningful situations. Holistic scoring of student responses gives a global picture of reading and writing performance.

Holistic Reading Assessment
Six Holistic Reading Assessments correlated to themes in the student anthologies are also available at each level of the program. Based on authentic reading selections, these assessments use a combination of multiple-choice and open-ended items to evaluate reading comprehension. A single, holistic score provides a snapshot of how students are progressing in the program.

Skills Assessment
Six Skills Assessments are available at each level of the program. They assess the major reading skills of decoding, vocabulary, comprehension, literary appreciation, and study skills, and the major grammar skills taught in *Signatures*. At grades 1 and 2, a separate

Harcourt Brace School Publishers • Skills Assessment

Phonemic Awareness Interview provides an informal assessment of a child's level of phonemic awareness to help the teacher plan for the development of literacy activities. The Skills Assessments may be used to diagnose students who are exhibiting difficulties or to evaluate progress in skills instruction.

Placement and Individual Inventory Teacher's Guide
This resource contains three assessment components. The Placement Test is a multiple-choice test that uses authentic reading selections similar to those the student will encounter in the program. It can be used individually or in large groups to estimate the appropriate level at which to place students.

The Emergent Literacy Assessment is an informal procedure for gathering information about a young child's past literacy experiences and for determining the appropriate placement in the program.

The Individual Diagnostic Inventory provides an additional tool for assessing a student's oral reading, comprehension, and writing. It may be used to diagnose strengths and weaknesses, to monitor progress in oral reading, and to evaluate instruction.

Portfolio Assessment Teacher's Guide
This assessment resource offers suggestions for initiating, maintaining, and evaluating student collections of reading and writing activities; guidelines and suggestions for conducting portfolio conferences; and ideas for sharing portfolios with parents, other teachers, and administrators. Also included in this Teacher's Guide are numerous suggestions and strategies for engaging students in self-assessment.

GENERAL ASSESSMENT CONSIDERATIONS

Description of the *Skills Assessments*

The *Skills Assessments* are criterion-referenced tests designed to measure students' achievement on the skills taught in *Signatures*. Criterion-referenced scores help teachers make decisions regarding the type of additional instruction that students may need.

Six *Skills Assessments* are available at this grade level—one assessment for each theme at Grade 5. Each *Skills Assessment* is composed of two major sections—one for Reading and one for Language Arts. The *Skills Assessment: Reading* evaluates students' achievement in decoding, vocabulary, comprehension, literary appreciation, and study skills. The *Skills Assessment: Language Arts* evaluates the grammar, mechanics, and usage skills taught in each theme. The formats used on the *Skills Assessments* follow the style and format presented in the Teacher's Edition and Practice Book. This ensures that the student is presented with familiar formats on the assessment and that the assessment measures only performance on skills.

Scheduling the Assessments

The *Skills Assessments* have been designed to correlate with specific skills introduced and reinforced within each theme of the program. Therefore, a *Skills Assessment* could be administered as a pretest before a theme is started to determine which skills needed to be emphasized. Or, a *Skills Assessment* could be administered after a theme is completed to verify that students can apply the skills that were taught.

The *Skills Assessment: Reading* and the *Skills Assessment: Language Arts* may be used independently, or in combination. That is, a teacher may choose to administer only the Reading portion of the *Skills Assessment*, only the Language Arts portion, or both the Reading and Language Arts sections, depending upon the goals of instruction and the purposes for assessing.

If possible, a *Skills Assessment: Reading* should be given in one session and a *Skills Assessment: Language Arts* should be given in one session. The tests are not timed. Most students should be able to complete either section in thirty to forty-five minutes.

Administering the Assessments

Prior to administering a *Skills Assessment*, the following general directions should be read to the students. **Say:**

We are going to do some special things today to find out how you are learning. We will be answering questions about some of the things we learned together in class. Do your very best and try to answer each of the questions.

Distribute the booklets and have students write their names on the Name line. When administering the assessment, repeat or clarify items that students do not hear or directions that they do not understand, but do not permit such explanations to reveal any answers.

Harcourt Brace School Publishers • Skills Assessment

SPECIFIC DIRECTIONS FOR ADMINISTERING SKILLS ASSESSMENT: READING

The directions for each assessment are printed on the pages of the student assessment booklets. There are no additional directions. If you wish, you may have students read the directions silently by themselves, or you may choose to read the directions aloud while students read them silently. If necessary, you may clarify any directions that students do not understand, as long as the clarification does not reveal any answers. Allow enough time for all students to complete the assessment or portion of the assessment being administered.

SPECIFIC DIRECTIONS FOR ADMINISTERING SKILLS ASSESSMENT: LANGUAGE ARTS

Prior to administering a *Skills Assessment: Language Arts,* you should give students general directions. Explain that they are going to answer questions to find out how well they understand and use the language skills they have been taught. Point out that some of the questions will be easy and others will be more difficult. Encourage students to do their best and to answer each question.

Follow these steps when administering a *Skills Assessment: Language Arts:*

1. Have each student write his or her name on the assessment booklet.

2. Help students locate the sample test page in their assessment booklets.

3. Identify the two kinds of questions students will encounter on the test: filling in a circle beside the correct answer, or an answer on the lines provided. Work through the sample items as a group. The first sample fill-in-the-circle question has been completed for the students. They complete the second fill-in-the-circle question independently. In the same way, the first sample write-in answer has been provided, and students complete the second one on their own. Discuss the correct answers to be sure students understand what they are to do.

4. After working the samples, point out the different parts of the assessment. Stress the importance of reading the directions before each section. Encourage students to work independently but to ask for help if they do not understand the directions.

5. Tell students to keep working until they come to the word "Stop." When they come to the word "Stop," they should put their pencils down and sit quietly until everyone is finished.

6. Monitor students as they work independently to make sure that they are following directions and answering items in the correct way.

Harcourt Brace School Publishers • Skills Assessment

SCORING AND INTERPRETING THE SKILLS ASSESSMENT: READING

The *Skills Assessment: Reading* can be scored in one of two ways. You may use either the annotated facsimile pages of the assessment booklets or the answer keys. Both can be found in this booklet. Follow these steps:

1. Open this booklet to the answer key or annotated facsimile page of the subtest to be scored.

2. Compare the student's responses, item by item, to the responses on the answer key and put a check mark next to each item that is correctly answered. It is recommended that you score the same subtest for all students before going on to score the next subtest. This method has been found to be more accurate and less time-consuming than scoring an entire assessment at one time.

3. Count the correct responses for the subtest and write this number on the Score line provided at the end of the subtest and on the booklet cover.

4. Continue this procedure for each subtest.

5. If you wish to evaluate a student's performance on a particular subtest, note which items measure that skill on the cover of the test booklet, and score that particular subtest. The number possible and the number needed to reach criterion are listed next to the line for the pupil score.

A student who scores at or above the criterion level for each subtest is considered competent in that skill area and is probably ready to move forward without addi-tional practice. A column for writing comments about "Pupil Strength" has been provided on the cover of the assessment booklet.

A student who does not reach criterion level probably needs additional instruction and/or practice. See the "Reading Skill Prescriptions for Reteaching" section of this booklet for more information.

A student's score on each skill or objective is a good estimate of how that student would perform on all possible items related to that objective. Enter a student's scores for all subtests on the Student Record Form found in this booklet. Criterion-referenced test scores should provide information you can use to plan instruction. Examine the student's scores for each subtest and decide whether you should "Move Forward" or "Reteach." Place an **M** or **R** in the "Diagnostic Category" (**DC**) column to record your decision.

Move Forward means that the student has reached the criterion level for a skill, and reading instruction can move forward. For example, on a subtest where there are 12 items, if the student scores 9 correct, and the criterion score for the subtest is 9/12, the student will receive **M** for **Move Forward**. This means that the student should be given practice in sustained reading to apply that particular reading skill. It does not mean that the student will never encounter any difficulty with that skill, nor does it mean that the skill is totally mastered. It does mean that the student seems to be quite good at that skill and should be given the opportunity to apply the skill to actual reading activities.

Harcourt Brace School Publishers • Skills Assessment

Reteach means that the student did not reach the criterion level for that skill. The student encountered difficulty with the skill and may have trouble understanding the skill. You should provide extra teaching on this skill with this student. The extra teaching may often be quite brief and may be accomplished through the skill prescriptions found in this booklet. Usually the student will need just a bit of extra guidance from you, accompanied by specific practice on the skill.

If a student scores at the **Reteach** level on only one of the test objectives, you may want to take the time to reteach that skill. The student may be grouped with other students who have experienced similar difficulty with that skill. However, when only one skill area is low, the student may have merely misunderstood the test directions or inadvertently forgotten to do several questions. If a student scores at the **Reteach** level on just one of the test objec-

tives, the student should not have any great difficulty moving on to the next theme. If a student scored at the **Reteach** level on two objectives, the student should definitely be given extra help as he or she moves on to the next theme.

If a student scored at the **Reteach** level on more than two objectives, the student may need a considerable amount of extra help. Moving that student along without extra help might cause more problems since the student is almost certain to encounter frustration in learning to read.

The *Skills Assessment: Reading* is just one observation of a student's reading behavior. It should be combined with other evidence of a student's progress, such as the teacher's daily observations, student work samples, and individual reading conferences. The sum of all of this information, coupled with test scores, is more reliable and valid than any single piece of information.

SCORING AND INTERPRETING THE SKILLS ASSESSMENT: LANGUAGE ARTS

Like the *Skills Assessment: Reading*, the *Skills Assessment: Language Arts* can be scored in one of two ways. You may use either the annotated facsimile pages of the assessment booklets or the answer keys. Both can be found in this booklet.

Unlike the *Skills Assessment: Reading*, the *Skills Assessment: Language Arts* is designed to yield a single, total score. Follow these steps to arrive at the total score:

1. Open this booklet to the answer key or

annotated facsimile page of the subtest to be scored.

2. Compare the student's responses, item by item, to the responses on the answer key and put a check mark next to each item that is correctly answered.

3. After each subtest has been scored, count the total number of correct responses for the entire assessment and write this number on the Student Record Form (see Appendix).

4. Use the following table to interpret the student's total score.

A student who scores at or above the criterion level for the total assessment is considered competent in the skills that were assessed and is probably ready to move forward without additional practice. A student who does not reach criterion level probably needs additional instruction and/or practice.

There are 12, 16, or 20 items on each *Skills Assessment: Language Arts*. For each item, a correct answer should be given 1 point, and an incorrect or missing answer should be given 0 points. Thus, a perfect score would be 12 (if 12 items), 16 (if 16 items), or 20 (if 20 items). Score ranges should be interpreted as follows:

Score (if 12 items)	Score (if 16 items)	Score (if 20 items)	Interpretation	Teaching Suggestions
9–12	12–16	15–20	Very good to excellent understanding and use of language skills	Students scoring at this level should have no difficulty moving forward to the next unit of language instruction.
7-8	10-11	12-14	Average understanding and use of language skills	Students scoring at this level may need a little extra help.
5-6	8-9	9-11	Fair understanding and use of language skills	Students scoring at this level should receive extra help. Note whether performance varied across the skills tested. Examine other samples of students' work to confirm their progress and pinpoint instructional needs.
0–4	0–7	0–8	Limited understanding and use of language skills	Students scoring at this level will almost certainly have difficulty completing this unit.

As with all tests, it is important not to place too much faith in a single test. The *Skills Assessment: Language Arts* provides only one sample of a student's language skills. This sample should be compared with the information you have gathered from daily observations, work samples, and perhaps other test scores.

Harcourt Brace School Publishers • Skills Assessment

READING SKILL PRESCRIPTIONS
FOR RETEACHING

COAST TO COAST / THEME **1**			
Skill	**Criterion Score**	**TE**	**PB**
VOCABULARY: Key Words	12/16	T19, T57, T79, T109, T135, T169	3, 10, 18
COMPREHENSION: Sequence and Cause and Effect	6/8	T58-T59, T85, T141, T259, R5	8–9, 17, 24

Harcourt Brace School Publishers • Skills Assessment

READING SKILL PRESCRIPTIONS
FOR RETEACHING

COAST TO COAST / THEME 2			
Skill	**Criterion Score**	**TE**	**PB**
VOCABULARY: Key Words	9/12	T213, T241, T253, T285, T299, T325, T343, T381	25, 32, 40, 49
COMPREHENSION: Make Predictions/Draw Conclusions	3/4	T242–T243, T263, T351, R41	30, 39, 55
COMPREHENSION: Fact and Opinion/Author's Purpose and Viewpoint	6/8	T286–287, T303, T305, T357, T917, R43	37–38, 47–48, 56

Harcourt Brace School Publishers • Skills Assessment

Reading Skill Prescriptions
for Reteaching

Coast to Coast / Theme 3			
Skill	**Criterion Score**	**TE**	**PB**
VOCABULARY: Key Words	9/12	T427, T461, T473, T503, T517, T547, T571, T613	57, 65, 73, 81
LITERARY APPRECIATION: Narrative Elements (Plot, setting, characters, theme)	6/8	T504–T505, T531, T585, R91	70–71, 80, 86
STUDY SKILLS: Reference Sources	3/4	T462–T468, T483, T527, R89	61–62, 72, 79

Harcourt Brace School Publishers • Skills Assessment

READING SKILL PRESCRIPTIONS FOR RETEACHING

COAST TO COAST / THEME 4			
Skill	**Criterion Score**	**TE**	**PB**
VOCABULARY: Key Words	9/12	T659, T689, T701, T733, T747, T775, T787, T813, T825, T863	89, 95, 102, 108, 117
VOCABULARY: Context Clues/Multiple- Meaning Words	6/8	T734–T735, T753, T837, R7	99–100, 107, 124
COMPREHENSION: Compare and Contrast	3/4	T690–T691, T709, T795, R5	93–94, 107, 115

Harcourt Brace School Publishers • Skills Assessment

READING SKILL PRESCRIPTIONS
FOR RETEACHING

		COAST TO COAST / THEME 5	
Skill	**Criterion Score**	**TE**	**PB**
DECODING: Structural Analysis (Prefixes, Suffixes, Roots)	6/8	T970–T971, T991, T1033, R69	136–137, 146, 154
VOCABULARY: Key Words	9/12	T907, T933, T945, T969, T983, T1009, T1029, T1059	125, 131, 139, 147
COMPREHENSION: Main Idea and Details	3/4	T934–T935, T951, T987, R67	129–130, 138, 145

READING SKILL PRESCRIPTIONS
FOR RETEACHING

COAST TO COAST / THEME 6			
Skill	Criterion Score	TE	PB
VOCABULARY: Key Words	12/16	T1099, T1125, T1137, T1165, T1179, T1213, T1225, T1249	155, 163, 171, 179
COMPREHENSION: Summarize/Paraphrase	6/8	T1126–T1127, T1166–T1167, T1195, T1229, R117, R119	160–161, 167–168, 178, 187

Harcourt Brace School Publishers • Skills Assessment

REDUCED AND ANNOTATED PUPIL EDITION FACSIMILE PAGES

COAST TO COAST / THEME 1

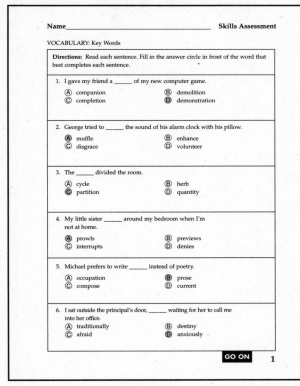

Name_____ Skills Assessment

VOCABULARY: Key Words

Directions: Read each sentence. Fill in the answer circle in front of the word that best completes each sentence.

1. I gave my friend a _____ of my new computer game.
   - Ⓐ companion
   - Ⓑ demolition
   - Ⓒ completion
   - Ⓓ demonstration

2. George tried to _____ the sound of his alarm clock with his pillow.
   - Ⓐ muffle
   - Ⓑ enhance
   - Ⓒ disgrace
   - Ⓓ volunteer

3. The _____ divided the room.
   - Ⓐ cycle
   - Ⓑ herb
   - Ⓒ partition
   - Ⓓ quantity

4. My little sister _____ around my bedroom when I'm not at home.
   - Ⓐ prowls
   - Ⓑ previews
   - Ⓒ interrupts
   - Ⓓ denies

5. Michael prefers to write _____ instead of poetry.
   - Ⓐ occupation
   - Ⓑ prose
   - Ⓒ compose
   - Ⓓ current

6. I sat outside the principal's door, _____ waiting for her to call me into her office.
   - Ⓐ traditionally
   - Ⓑ destiny
   - Ⓒ afraid
   - Ⓓ anxiously

GO ON 1

Name_____ Skills Assessment

VOCABULARY: Key Words (continued)

7. Sarah tried to sound _____ when she told her friend about her part in the school play.
   - Ⓐ despair
   - Ⓑ interrupted
   - Ⓒ nonchalant
   - Ⓓ shriveled

8. _____ such as being able to watch television are earned through good behavior.
   - Ⓐ Privileges
   - Ⓑ Pledges
   - Ⓒ Instincts
   - Ⓓ Qualities

9. After I told my brother I'd lost all my money, he said _____ , "You are so responsible."
   - Ⓐ hostility
   - Ⓑ sarcastically
   - Ⓒ unreliable
   - Ⓓ noticeably

10. I will be the _____ of the fifth grade if I wear my shoes on the wrong feet again.
    - Ⓐ laughingstock
    - Ⓑ bulldozer
    - Ⓒ amateur
    - Ⓓ embarrass

11. After he robbed the bank, the _____ escaped.
    - Ⓐ custom
    - Ⓑ defiant
    - Ⓒ expression
    - Ⓓ culprit

12. Our dog was _____ at Grandma's feet, begging her to give him one more bone.
    - Ⓐ groveling
    - Ⓑ concealing
    - Ⓒ cautiously
    - Ⓓ disguising

2 **GO ON**

Harcourt Brace School Publishers • Skills Assessment

Name_____ Skills Assessment

VOCABULARY: Key Words (continued)

13. I _____ every time I see a mouse.
    - Ⓐ mimic
    - Ⓑ supply
    - Ⓒ cringe
    - Ⓓ resemble

14. The boat's _____ was broken, so we couldn't go out on the lake.
    - Ⓐ property
    - Ⓑ recovery
    - Ⓒ propeller
    - Ⓓ chisel

15. When my cousin had _____ , he was in the hospital.
    - Ⓐ pneumonia
    - Ⓑ scientist
    - Ⓒ javelin
    - Ⓓ neutral

16. Amanda was so _____ she could barely speak.
    - Ⓐ coiled
    - Ⓑ jubilation
    - Ⓒ offhanded
    - Ⓓ flustered

STOP! 3

Name_____ Skills Assessment

COMPREHENSION: Sequence/Cause and Effect

Directions: Read each passage. Fill in the answer circle in front of the correct answer for each question.

Heather and her mother decided to bake cookies. First, they made a list of ingredients they needed and then drove to the store. When they got home, to save time, Heather preheated the oven while her mother placed things on the counter. Then, Heather measured and mixed dry ingredients while her mom greased the cookie sheets. Next, Heather cracked eggs into a separate bowl and added all the remaining ingredients. She mixed half the ingredients with a blender. Slowly, Heather added the dry ingredients to the egg mixture. Finally, it was time to add the chocolate chips. Then, Heather dropped balls of dough onto a cookie sheet and put it in the oven. The smell of baking cookies drew Heather's father into the kitchen. A few minutes later, they all ate freshly baked cookies and drank milk.

17. Why did Heather and her mother make a list before going to the store?
    - Ⓐ They wanted to bake cookies.
    - Ⓑ Heather wanted chocolate chips.
    - Ⓒ To make sure they had all the ingredients.
    - Ⓓ They were out of milk.

18. While Heather preheated the oven, her mother _____ .
    - Ⓐ called her father to the kitchen
    - Ⓑ cracked the eggs
    - Ⓒ dropped balls of dough onto a cookie sheet
    - Ⓓ placed things on the counter

19. Heather added the chocolate chips before _____ .
    - Ⓐ she preheated the oven
    - Ⓑ her mom greased the cookie sheets
    - Ⓒ her father came into the kitchen
    - Ⓓ she used the blender

20. Why did Heather's father come into the kitchen?
    - Ⓐ He wanted to talk to Heather.
    - Ⓑ He smelled baking cookies.
    - Ⓒ Heather called him.
    - Ⓓ He wanted to bake cookies.

4 **GO ON**

COMPREHENSION: Sequence/Cause and Effect (continued)

David's mom asked him to go to the grocery store after school to buy bread, potatoes, lettuce, and cheese.

"Make a list so you won't forget anything," she suggested.

"Don't worry, Mom. I'll remember," David replied.

David went to the grocery store. He bought the potatoes, lettuce, and cheese and then went home. That's when David realized he should have made a list after all. He'd have to go back to the store for the bread.

21. When did David go to the store?

Ⓐ after school
Ⓑ before he went to school
Ⓒ when his homework was done
Ⓓ after he did his chores around the house

22. Why couldn't David's mother make him a cheese sandwich when he got home?

Ⓐ She thought it would spoil his dinner.
Ⓑ She was out of cheese.
Ⓒ She was out of bread.
Ⓓ He wasn't hungry.

GO ON   5

COMPREHENSION: Sequence/Cause and Effect (continued)

Eric was surprised when his older sister Nina invited him to go to a movie with her and her friends. Eric was nervous and excited about going to a movie with the older kids. While he was getting ready, he decided he didn't like the pants he was wearing, so he changed into a new pair.

At the movie theater, Eric reached for his wallet, but it wasn't there. "Oh, no," he thought. "What happened to my wallet? Where could it be?"

Just then Nina said, "Eric, I'm glad you could come with us. I never did thank you properly for helping me clean the family room for my party, so I'd like to pay for your movie ticket."

23. Because Eric helped Nina clean the family room, _____ .

Ⓐ Nina bought Eric a new pair of pants
Ⓑ Nina helped Eric paint his room
Ⓒ Nina treated Eric to a movie
Ⓓ Nina gave a party for Eric

24. When did Eric realize he didn't have his wallet with him?

Ⓐ When he was thinking about going to the movies.
Ⓑ After he got to the movie theater.
Ⓒ When his sister paid for his ticket.
Ⓓ When he changed into a new pair of pants.

STOP!

6

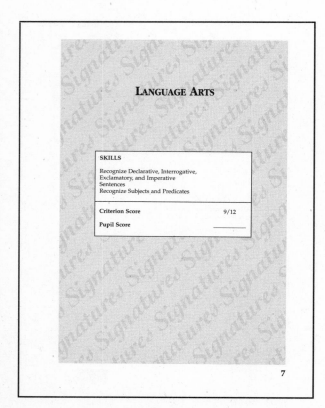

LANGUAGE ARTS

SKILLS

Recognize Declarative, Interrogative, Exclamatory, and Imperative Sentences
Recognize Subjects and Predicates

Criterion Score	9/12
Pupil Score	_____

7

Sample Multiple-Choice Questions:

The first kind of question is multiple choice. Carefully read the directions and the question. Then fill in the answer circle beside the choice you think is best. Question 1 has been answered for you. Look at it and then answer question 2.

Directions: Choose the **complete subject** of each sentence.

1. Tom ran to school.
Ⓐ Tom
Ⓑ ran

2. The cat slept on the chair.
Ⓐ The cat
Ⓑ slept on the chair

Sample Write-in-the-Answer Questions:

For the second kind of question, carefully read the directions and the question. Then write your answer on the line. Question 3 has been answered for you. Look at it and then answer question 4.

Directions: Write the **complete predicate** of each sentence.

3. We went to the ball game.
   went to the ball game

4. The game was exciting.
   was exciting

8

Harcourt Brace School Publishers • Skills Assessment

Directions: Decide whether each sentence is **declarative, interrogative, exclamatory,** or **imperative.** Fill in the answer circle beside the one you choose.

1. Who ate the last piece of chocolate cake?
   Ⓐ declarative
   Ⓑ interrogative
   Ⓒ exclamatory
   Ⓓ imperative

2. I didn't even get a piece of cake.
   Ⓐ declarative
   Ⓑ interrogative
   Ⓒ exclamatory
   Ⓓ imperative

3. I didn't take it!
   Ⓐ declarative
   Ⓑ interrogative
   Ⓒ exclamatory
   Ⓓ imperative

4. Mom bought the cake Monday morning.
   Ⓐ declarative
   Ⓑ interrogative
   Ⓒ exclamatory
   Ⓓ imperative

GO ON   9

---

5. What did your teacher tell you?
   Ⓐ declarative
   Ⓑ interrogative
   Ⓒ exclamatory
   Ⓓ imperative

6. Don't drop that box.
   Ⓐ declarative
   Ⓑ interrogative
   Ⓒ exclamatory
   Ⓓ imperative

7. How cold that water is!
   Ⓐ declarative
   Ⓑ interrogative
   Ⓒ exclamatory
   Ⓓ imperative

8. Pass me the scissors.
   Ⓐ declarative
   Ⓑ interrogative
   Ⓒ exclamatory
   Ⓓ imperative

10   GO ON

COAST TO COAST / THEME 2

Directions: Write the **subject** of this sentence.

9. Fish darted in and out of the shallows.

fish _____

Directions: Write the complete **predicate** of this sentence.

10. The chickens huddled together for warmth.

huddled together for warmth _____

Directions: Tell whether the **subject** or the **predicate** is missing from each sentence.

11. Was going to get his way, no matter what.

subject _____

12. Tommy and the guys from his baseball team.

predicate _____

STOP!   11

VOCABULARY: Key Words

Directions: Read each sentence. Fill in the answer circle in front of the word that best completes each sentence.

1. When I get home from school, I like to relax in my _____ .
   Ⓐ heritage   Ⓑ hammock
   Ⓒ current   Ⓓ exhibit

2. Since no one paid attention to me, I felt as though I were _____ .
   Ⓐ conscious   Ⓑ recovery
   Ⓒ invisible   Ⓓ mechanical

3. Receiving a phone call from my favorite uncle made my birthday very _____ .
   Ⓐ memorable   Ⓑ impatient
   Ⓒ celebration   Ⓓ indifferent

4. The weary _____ came ashore after months at sea.
   Ⓐ mergers   Ⓑ mariners
   Ⓒ frontiers   Ⓓ expressions

5. The _____ for our trip were put on the boat before we left.
   Ⓐ provisions   Ⓑ festivities
   Ⓒ splendid   Ⓓ inspiration

6. The principal _____ the school's new flag for all to see.
   Ⓐ unfurled   Ⓑ rebuilt
   Ⓒ emerges   Ⓓ ignored

GO ON   1

VOCABULARY: Key Words (continued)

7. The _____ cheered their team to victory.
   - (A) surroundings
   - (B) determination
   - (C) sleighs
   - (D) spectators

8. The teacher _____ the students' request to hold class outdoors.
   - (A) illustrated
   - (B) convinced
   - (C) vetoed
   - (D) transmits

9. She has the _____ to make many of her own decisions.
   - (A) loyalty
   - (B) liberty
   - (C) independent
   - (D) oppression

10. My uncle's apple trees _____ a huge crop each year.
    - (A) descend
    - (B) quantity
    - (C) compose
    - (D) yield

11. Caroline consulted two _____ to find out the population of the United States.
    - (A) almanacs
    - (B) inquiries
    - (C) despots
    - (D) improvisations

12. _____ the mystery of the missing lunch money was a difficult undertaking.
    - (A) Engineering
    - (B) Positioning
    - (C) Universal
    - (D) Unraveling

2   **STOP!**

COMPREHENSION: Make Predictions/Draw Conclusions

Directions: Read each passage. Fill in the answer circle in front of the correct answer for each question.

Sarah and Timothy planned to go horseback riding with their father on Sunday afternoon, but they had to finish their homework first. On Sunday morning Timothy began working on a book report that was due Monday. After finishing the first paragraph, he realized that the report was going to take him longer to write than he had thought. That afternoon Timothy was still working on his report when it was time to drive out to the stables. Sarah grabbed her coat and ran outside to meet her father, who was waiting in his truck.

13. What can you conclude about how Timothy spent Sunday afternoon?
    - (A) He played in the back of his father's truck.
    - (B) He worked with Sarah to finish his book report.
    - (C) He finished writing his book report alone.
    - (D) He went riding with Sarah and his father.

14. From this passage, you might predict that _____ .
    - (A) Timothy will never write another book report again.
    - (B) Sarah will go riding with her father on Monday.
    - (C) The horses will be tired when Sarah and her father arrive at the stables.
    - (D) Timothy will allow more time to write book reports in the future.

                                                            GO ON   3

COMPREHENSION: Make Predictions/Draw Conclusions (continued)

Mrs. Halloway, the lunch monitor at Washington Elementary School, made sure the lunch room ran smoothly. She did not get too upset when things got a little noisy or something spilled, but she would not tolerate littering. If she saw a student drop something without picking it up, she'd walk up to that person and insist that he or she pick up the item and throw it in the trash can.

Mike and Toby were heading for their usual table. Mike was trying to carry his lunch tray in one hand and some books in the other. A napkin flew off his tray and landed on the floor. Mike didn't even notice it, but Mrs. Halloway did.

15. Mike and Toby probably _____ .
    - (A) look alike
    - (B) live on the same street
    - (C) ride the school bus together
    - (D) eat lunch together every day

16. From this passage you can predict that Mrs. Halloway will _____ .
    - (A) change Mike's and Toby's seats
    - (B) tell Mike to pick up the napkin
    - (C) ask Toby to stay after school
    - (D) punish Toby for making too much noise during lunch

4   **STOP!**

COMPREHENSION: Fact and Opinion/Author's Purpose and Viewpoint

Directions: Read each passage. Fill in the answer circle in front of the correct answer for each question.

Many people think that George Herman "Babe" Ruth was the greatest baseball player of all time. He set many records. For example, he hit 714 home runs during his career, and 60 in a single season. When he first started playing, he was a pitcher, and he set several pitching records. Later he became an outfielder and one of the most legendary hitters of all times. He was also an interesting and colorful character who was known for visiting sick children in hospitals and doing other kind deeds. However, he had a very difficult childhood and suffered from illnesses later in his life. Still, most people remember him as a great American hero. Although some of his records have since been broken, others still stand.

17. Which sentence states an opinion from the passage?
    - (A) He was a great American hero.
    - (B) He hit 60 home runs in a single season.
    - (C) When he started playing, he was a pitcher.
    - (D) His real name was George Herman Ruth.

18. The author wrote this paragraph to _____ .
    - (A) entertain
    - (B) inform
    - (C) persuade
    - (D) give directions

                                                            GO ON   5

Harcourt Brace School Publishers • Skills Assessment

COMPREHENSION: Fact and Opinion/Author's Purpose and Viewpoint (continued)

On July 29, 1993 my cat Fluffy had a litter of five kittens. They were all beautiful, but one was much smaller than the others. It was also weaker than the other four and usually didn't get much milk from its mother because the other kittens kept pushing it away. My mother suggested feeding it with a baby bottle. We took great care of this little kitten that had become our favorite. After several weeks the little kitten had grown stronger. We named her Joy because we enjoyed her so much, and now, several years later, we still think Joy is the best cat in the world.

19. Which sentence states a **fact** from the passage?

   Ⓐ All of Fluffy's kittens were beautiful.
   Ⓑ Joy is the best cat in the world.
   Ⓒ The other kittens were jealous of Joy.
   Ⓓ The kittens were born on July 29.

20. The author's purpose in this passage was to _____.

   Ⓐ inform
   Ⓑ persuade
   Ⓒ entertain
   Ⓓ give directions

6   **GO ON**

COMPREHENSION: Fact and Opinion/Author's Purpose and Viewpoint (continued)

Carrie wanted to buy a special sweater for her mother's birthday, but she didn't have enough money. As Carrie walked home from school, she saw a wallet on the ground. She picked it up and looked inside. There were fifty dollars in the wallet! That was more than enough to buy her mother the beautiful sweater she had seen in the store window. Then Carrie looked through the rest of the wallet and found a driver's license. It belonged to Fred Blackwell and showed his address — 4286 South Oak Street. South Oak Street was right across the street. Carrie suddenly realized she couldn't keep the wallet. She crossed the street and rang the doorbell. A man answered the door, and Carrie asked, "Are you Mr. Blackwell?" The man said he was, and Carrie handed him his wallet. Mr. Blackwell was so happy to have his wallet back that he gave Carrie twenty dollars. Now Carrie could afford the beautiful sweater for her mother.

21. Which sentence states an **opinion** from the passage?

   Ⓐ Carrie saw a beautiful sweater in a store window.
   Ⓑ Carrie saw a wallet on the ground.
   Ⓒ Mr. Blackwell lives at 4286 South Oak Street.
   Ⓓ The wallet belonged to Fred Blackwell.

22. The author of this story probably believes that, _____.

   Ⓐ "Easy does it."
   Ⓑ "Honesty is the best policy."
   Ⓒ "Finders keepers; losers weepers."
   Ⓓ "Every man for himself."

       GO ON 7

COMPREHENSION: Fact and Opinion/Author's Purpose and Viewpoint (continued)

Monica was one of six finalists in the sixth-grade spelling bee. She expected the spelling words in the final round to be very difficult. On the way to the final competition, Monica's father told her that he and her mother were very proud of her and that, win or lose in today's contest, she would always be the best in their eyes. Monica believed she had the greatest parents in the world. She knew all they expected of her was that she do her best.

23. Which sentence states a **fact** from the passage?

   Ⓐ Monica was an excellent speller.
   Ⓑ There were six finalists in the spelling bee.
   Ⓒ Monica had the greatest parents in the world.
   Ⓓ The spelling words in the final round were very difficult.

24. The author of this passage wants the reader to know _____.

   Ⓐ how to study spelling words
   Ⓑ how hard it is to win a spelling bee
   Ⓒ how important it is to be good at spelling
   Ⓓ how Monica and her parents feel about each other

8   **STOP!**

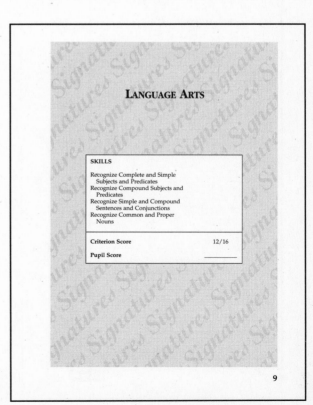

LANGUAGE ARTS

SKILLS

Recognize Complete and Simple
  Subjects and Predicates
Recognize Compound Subjects and
  Predicates
Recognize Simple and Compound
  Sentences and Conjunctions
Recognize Common and Proper
  Nouns

Criterion Score	12/16
Pupil Score	_____

9

Page 10

Sample Multiple-Choice Questions:

The first kind of question is multiple choice. Carefully read the directions and the question. Then fill in the answer circle beside the choice you think is best. Question 1 has been answered for you. Look at it and then answer question 2.

Directions: Choose the **complete subject** of each sentence.

1. Tom ran to school.
   - Ⓐ Tom
   - Ⓑ ran

2. The cat slept on the chair.
   - Ⓐ The cat
   - Ⓑ slept on the chair

Sample Write-in-the-Answer Questions:

For the second kind of question, carefully read the directions and the question. Then write your answer on the line. Question 3 has been answered for you. Look at it and then answer question 4.

Directions: Write the **complete predicate** of each sentence.

3. We went to the ball game.
   went to the ball game

4. The game was exciting.
   was exciting

10

Page 11

Directions: Choose the **simple subject** of this sentence. Fill in the answer circle beside the one you choose.

1. The stone walls around the garden were old and crumbling.
   - Ⓐ stone
   - Ⓑ walls
   - Ⓒ garden

Directions: Choose the **simple predicate** of this sentence. Fill in the answer circle beside the one you choose.

2. Ferns grew in the shade.
   - Ⓐ grew
   - Ⓑ grew shade
   - Ⓒ grew in the shade

Directions: Write the **complete predicate** of this sentence.

3. The cherry tree blossoms were falling like snow.
   were falling like snow

Directions: Write the **complete subject** of this sentence.

4. Red and white tulips bobbed in the warm spring breeze.
   red and white tulips

Directions: Decide whether each sentence has a **compound subject** or a **compound predicate.** Fill in the answer circle beside the one you choose.

5. The ducks and geese walked in single file down to the river.
   - Ⓐ compound subject
   - Ⓑ compound predicate

6. Rubber cement does a neater job and is much quicker.
   - Ⓐ compound subject
   - Ⓑ compound predicate

GO ON   11

Page 12

Directions: Write the **compound subject** of each sentence.

7. Swimming and sailing are my favorite water sports.
   swimming, sailing

8. The children and their friends called and called.
   children, friends

Directions: Decide whether each sentence is a **simple sentence** or a **compound sentence.** Fill in the answer circle beside the one you choose.

9. Somebody left this book, but I don't know who it was.
   - Ⓐ simple sentence
   - Ⓑ compound sentence

10. Perhaps the owner of the book doesn't want it back.
    - Ⓐ simple sentence
    - Ⓑ compound sentence

Directions: Write the two **simple sentences** that form this compound sentence.

11. Ask Julie the question, but she might not know the answer.
    Ask Julie the question.
    She might not know the answer.

Directions: Write the **conjunction** that joins these two simple sentences.

12. Mark brought the sandwiches, or maybe he helped with the salad.
    _or_

12   GO ON

Page 13

Directions: Choose the **proper noun** to complete this sentence. Fill in the answer circle beside the one you choose.

13. Someone did a report on _____ .
    - Ⓐ sand sharks
    - Ⓑ William Shakespeare

Directions: Decide whether all the nouns in this sentence are **proper nouns** or **common nouns.** Fill in the answer circle beside the one you choose.

14. The Wilsons visited Washington in March.
    - Ⓐ proper nouns
    - Ⓑ common nouns

Directions: Write the **common nouns** in this sentence.

15. His grandmother left for her home in Georgia last Tuesday.
    grandmother, home

Directions: Write the **proper nouns** in this sentence.

16. Old Faithful is the name of a geyser at Yellowstone National Park.
    Old Faithful, Yellowstone National Park

STOP!   13

T20

Harcourt Brace School Publishers • Skills Assessment

Name_____ Skills Assessment

VOCABULARY: Key Words

Directions: Read each sentence. Fill in the answer circle in front of the word that best completes each sentence.

1. The thief was caught _____ goods across the border.
   - (A) prospecting
   - (B) distinguishing
   - (C) frequenting
   - (D) smuggling

2. My father warned us to stay away from the old, _____ house.
   - (A) oppressed
   - (B) condemned
   - (C) constant
   - (D) satisfied

3. I marked off my _____ by drawing a circle in the sand.
   - (A) territory
   - (B) settler
   - (C) recovery
   - (D) shade

4. My parents are going to listen to the presidential _____ .
   - (A) occupation
   - (B) convince
   - (C) superior
   - (D) address

5. My aunt is trying to _____ a summer camp for children.
   - (A) establish
   - (B) invest
   - (C) evidence
   - (D) escape

6. Mark and his sister explored the college _____ together.
   - (A) supply
   - (B) conceal
   - (C) campus
   - (D) patrol

GO ON 1

Name_____ Skills Assessment

VOCABULARY: Key Words (continued)

7. The woman's _____ to the school was very generous.
   - (A) impression
   - (B) donation
   - (C) debut
   - (D) talent

8. Tracy _____ the house for her book, but she couldn't find it anywhere.
   - (A) rated
   - (B) furiously
   - (C) paid
   - (D) scoured

9. Paul mixed a _____ of mud, sand, and leaves in a bucket.
   - (A) rustle
   - (B) scenery
   - (C) theory
   - (D) concoction

10. Annie successfully _____ her bicycle through the tricky course.
    - (A) maneuvered
    - (B) flew
    - (C) cautiously
    - (D) survived

11. Although the instructions were _____ , Billy was able to build the model airplane.
    - (A) noticeable
    - (B) dreaded
    - (C) supervised
    - (D) vague

12. After the flood _____ , people returned to their homes.
    - (A) despaired
    - (B) disrupted
    - (C) abated
    - (D) improvised

2 **STOP!**

Name_____ Skills Assessment

LITERARY APPRECIATION: Narrative elements

Directions: Read each passage. Fill in the answer circle in front of the correct answer for each question.

Richard and his father sat on a dock by the lake near their campsite. They were hoping to catch fish for supper. However, neither of them had ever fished before, and they were not sure how to do it. Richard's father took a worm and tried wrapping it around his hook. Every time he thought the worm was on the hook, the worm fell off. Richard tried too, with the same unhappy results.

After a while they decided they needed some help. They walked along the edge of the lake in search of other campers, but the area was so vast and secluded that they never found anyone. Fishing would have to wait for another camping trip. Richard and his father returned to their tent site and unpacked sandwiches and chips from a bag. Richard was glad his mother had insisted on sending food.

13. The main characters in this story are a boy and his _____ .
    - (A) mother
    - (B) father
    - (C) brother
    - (D) friend

14. The beginning of this story takes place _____ .
    - (A) on a dock
    - (B) on a boat
    - (C) on an island
    - (D) in a field

15. The plot of this story is mostly about _____ .
    - (A) how to find worms
    - (B) the hazards of camping
    - (C) family relationships
    - (D) unsuccessful fishermen

16. Which is the best statement of the theme of this story?
    - (A) "Be prepared."
    - (B) "Never tell a lie."
    - (C) "Things could always be worse."
    - (D) "You can't teach an old dog new tricks."

GO ON 3

Name_____ Skills Assessment

LITERARY APPRECIATION: Narrative Elements (continued)

Kisha was babysitting little Ivan, the first infant she'd ever watched alone. Ivan's parents had gone to dinner and a show and would be home late. Everything started out fine. Kisha fed Ivan. Then she held the baby in her arms, rocked him, and sang to him. After Ivan fell asleep, she put him in his crib. Suddenly, however, Ivan woke up crying. Kisha picked him up and tried to calm him down. She sang more songs to him and bounced him in her arms, but nothing worked.

Finally Kisha called her mother. She told her mother everything she had tried. Her mother listened patiently and then asked, "Have you changed his diaper tonight?" Kisha felt foolish. That was the problem. In five minutes Ivan was happy and dry.

17. The main characters in this story are Ivan and his _____ .
    - (A) father
    - (B) mother
    - (C) sister
    - (D) babysitter

18. This story takes place _____ .
    - (A) at Ivan's house
    - (B) in a restaurant
    - (C) at a show
    - (D) at a day care center

19. The plot of this story is mostly about how Kisha _____ .
    - (A) discovered Ivan's problem
    - (B) earned extra money
    - (C) helped her mother
    - (D) sang songs

20. Which is the best statement of the theme of this story?
    - (A) Rock-a-by baby.
    - (B) Mother knows best.
    - (C) You can't be too careful.
    - (D) Children should be seen and not heard.

4 **STOP!**

STUDY SKILLS: Reference Sources

Directions: Look at the set of encyclopedia. Then read the article. Fill in the answer circle in front of the correct answer for each question.

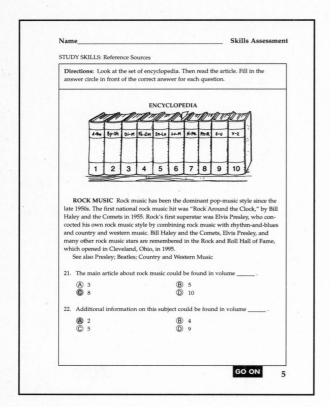

ENCYCLOPEDIA

A-Bu	By-Dh	Di-Fi	Fo-Jm	Jn-Lo	Lu-M	N-Pe	Ph-R	S-U	V-Z
1	2	3	4	5	6	7	8	9	10

   ROCK MUSIC Rock music has been the dominant pop-music style since the late 1950s. The first national rock music hit was "Rock Around the Clock," by Bill Haley and the Comets in 1955. Rock's first superstar was Elvis Presley, who concocted his own rock music style by combining rock music with rhythm-and-blues and country and western music. Bill Haley and the Comets, Elvis Presley, and many other rock music stars are remembered in the Rock and Roll Hall of Fame, which opened in Cleveland, Ohio, in 1995.
   See also Presley; Beatles; Country and Western Music

21. The main article about rock music could be found in volume _____ .
   Ⓐ 3   Ⓑ 5
   Ⓒ 8   Ⓓ 10

22. Additional information on this subject could be found in volume _____ .
   Ⓐ 2   Ⓑ 4
   Ⓒ 5   Ⓓ 9

GO ON   5

STUDY SKILLS: Reference Sources (continued)

Directions: Look at this part of a page from a dictionary. Then read the questions. Fill in the answer circle in front of the correct answer for each question.

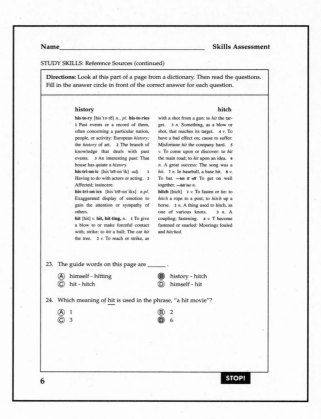

history

his·to·ry [his´tə-rē] *n., pl.* **his·to·ries** 1 Past events or a record of them, often concerning a particular nation, people, or activity: European *history;* the *history* of art. 2 The branch of knowledge that deals with past events. 3 An interesting past: That house has quiate a *history.*
his·tri·on·ic [his´trē-on´ik] *adj.* 1 Having to do with actors or acting. 2 Affected; insincere.
his·tri·on·ics [his´trē-on´iks] *n.pl.* Exaggerated display of emotion to gain the attention or sympathy of others.
hit [hit] *v.* **hit, hit·ting,** *n.* 1 To give a blow to or make forceful contact with; strike: to *hit* a ball; The car *hit* the tree. 2 *v.* To reach or strike, as

hitch

with a shot from a gun: to *hit* the target. 3 *n.* Something, as a blow or shot, that reaches its target. 4 *v.* To have a bad effect on; cause to suffer: Misfortune *hit* the company hard. 5 *v.* To come upon or discover: to *hit* the main road; to *hit* upon an idea. 6 *n.* A great success: The song was a *hit.* 7 *n.* In baseball, a base hit. 8 *v.* To bat. —**hit it off** To get on well together. —**hit´ter** *n.*
hitch [hich] 1 *v.* To fasten or tie: to *hitch* a rope to a post; to *hitch* up a horse. 2 *n.* A thing used to hitch, as one of various knots. 3 *n.* A coupling; fastening. 4 *v.* To become fastened or snarled: Moorings fouled and *hitched.*

23. The guide words on this page are _____ .
   Ⓐ himself - hitting   Ⓑ history - hitch
   Ⓒ hit - hitch   Ⓓ himself - hit

24. Which meaning of *hit* is used in the phrase, "a hit movie"?
   Ⓐ 1   Ⓑ 2
   Ⓒ 3   Ⓓ 6

STOP!

6

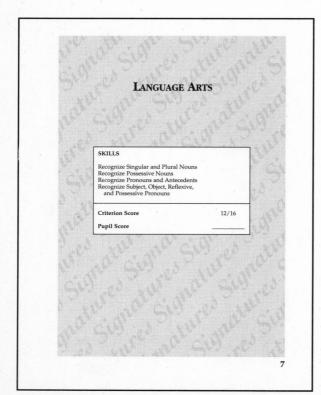

LANGUAGE ARTS

SKILLS

Recognize Singular and Plural Nouns
Recognize Possessive Nouns
Recognize Pronouns and Antecedents
Recognize Subject, Object, Reflexive,
   and Possessive Pronouns

Criterion Score	12/16
Pupil Score	_____

7

Sample Multiple-Choice Questions:

The first kind of question is multiple choice. Carefully read the directions and the question. Then fill in the answer circle beside the choice you think is best. Question 1 has been answered for you. Look at it and then answer question 2.

Directions: Choose the **complete subject** of each sentence.

1. Tom ran to school.
   Ⓐ Tom
   Ⓑ ran

2. The cat slept on the chair.
   Ⓐ The cat
   Ⓑ slept on the chair

Sample Write-in-the-Answer Questions:

For the second kind of question, carefully read the directions and the question. Then write your answer on the line. Question 3 has been answered for you. Look at it and then answer question 4.

Directions: Write the **complete predicate** of each sentence.

3. We went to the ball game.
   went to the ball game

4. The game was exciting.
   was exciting

8

Page 9

Name_____ Skills Assessment

Directions: Decide whether all the **nouns** in this sentence are **singular** or **plural**. Fill in the answer circle beside the one you choose.

1. Charla banged on the drum while her sister and brother sang.

  Ⓐ singular
  Ⓑ plural

Directions: Choose the **plural noun** in this sentence. Fill in the answer circle beside the one you choose.

2. The ducks walked down the hill and paddled across the lake.

  Ⓐ ducks
  Ⓑ hill
  Ⓒ lake

Directions: Write the **singular nouns** in this sentence.

3. His son could see three frogs on the bottom.

  son, bottom

Directions: Rewrite this sentence to make the **nouns plural**.

4. The robin perched on the branch.

  The robins perched on the branches.

GO ON 9

Page 10

Name_____ Skills Assessment

Directions: Choose the **possessive noun** in this sentence. Fill in the answer circle beside the one you choose.

5. I was surprised that she drove Mel's car.

  Ⓐ I
  Ⓑ she
  Ⓒ Mel's

Directions: Rewrite the **possessive nouns** in this sentence correctly.

6. The imprint on the childrens shirts said "Chicagos Best."

  children's, Chicago's

Directions: Choose the correct way to rewrite the underlined phrase in each sentence by using a **possessive noun**.

7. The manes of the horses were white with snow.

  Ⓐ horse's manes
  Ⓑ horses' manes
  Ⓒ horses mane's

8. There's gold at the end of the rainbow.

  Ⓐ the rainbows' end
  Ⓑ the rain bow's
  Ⓒ the rainbow's end

10 GO ON

Page 11

Name_____ Skills Assessment

Directions: Choose the **pronoun** that best replaces the underlined words in each sentence. Fill in the answer circle beside the one you choose.

9. Petra and J.R. wanted to borrow our bikes.

  Ⓐ Them
  Ⓑ Us
  Ⓒ They

10. That telephone call was for Rosa.

  Ⓐ her
  Ⓑ we
  Ⓒ his

Directions: Choose the **antecedent** of the **pronoun** in this sentence. Fill in the answer circle beside the one you choose.

11. Marshall wanted to go along, but he got home after Joy left.

  Ⓐ Marshall
  Ⓑ but
  Ⓒ Joy

Directions: Write the four **pronouns** in this sentence.

12. We weren't sure if he himself knew where to find them.

  We, he, himself, them

GO ON 11

Page 12

Name_____ Skills Assessment

Directions: Decide whether the underlined word is a **subject pronoun**, an **object pronoun**, a **reflexive pronoun**, or a **possessive pronoun**. Fill in the answer circle beside the one you choose.

13. We saw the plane go down ourselves.

  Ⓐ subject pronoun
  Ⓑ object pronoun
  Ⓒ reflexive pronoun
  Ⓓ possessive pronoun

14. He spent weeks in the wilderness.

  Ⓐ subject pronoun
  Ⓑ object pronoun
  Ⓒ reflexive pronoun
  Ⓓ possessive pronoun

Directions: Write the **object pronoun** in this sentence.

15. He realized that almost nothing scared him.

  him

Directions: Write the **subject pronoun** in this sentence.

16. We won't come until Nina herself calls us.

  We

12 STOP!

Name_____ Skills Assessment

VOCABULARY: Key Words

Directions: Read each sentence. Fill in the answer circle in front of the word that best completes each sentence.

1. The reporter focused her article _____ on the town's problems.
   - Ⓐ determination
   - Ⓑ horizontally
   - Ⓒ firm
   - Ⓓ exclusively

2. The dog did not bark because it was _____.
   - Ⓐ timidly
   - Ⓑ mute
   - Ⓒ oppression
   - Ⓓ noticeable

3. Lizzie was _____ the question by pretending not to have heard it.
   - Ⓐ evading
   - Ⓑ indicating
   - Ⓒ supervising
   - Ⓓ treatment

4. I don't like it when people try to _____ their beliefs on me.
   - Ⓐ appeal
   - Ⓑ haze
   - Ⓒ superior
   - Ⓓ impose

5. Dana _____ a class rule by calling out without raising her hand.
   - Ⓐ engaged
   - Ⓑ instigated
   - Ⓒ violated
   - Ⓓ stimulated

6. My dad used his _____ to convince people to vote for building a new school.
   - Ⓐ influence
   - Ⓑ rustle
   - Ⓒ conquer
   - Ⓓ inspection

GO ON   1

Name_____ Skills Assessment

VOCABULARY: Key Words (continued)

7. Nancy was so proud after her successful piano _____.
   - Ⓐ perform
   - Ⓑ culture
   - Ⓒ recital
   - Ⓓ veranda

8. My grandma _____ the bread dough with her hands.
   - Ⓐ enchanted
   - Ⓑ kneaded
   - Ⓒ complimented
   - Ⓓ resembled

9. Before I play a song on the piano, I always practice the _____.
   - Ⓐ scales
   - Ⓑ prodigies
   - Ⓒ improvise
   - Ⓓ characters

10. The robot had a _____ voice.
    - Ⓐ exhibition
    - Ⓑ dignity
    - Ⓒ peculiar
    - Ⓓ endangered

11. When he blows into that trumpet, he makes a _____ noise.
    - Ⓐ spiral
    - Ⓑ flax
    - Ⓒ dreadful
    - Ⓓ conscious

12. Your kind words were greatly _____.
    - Ⓐ talented
    - Ⓑ appreciated
    - Ⓒ indifferent
    - Ⓓ shriveled

2   STOP!

Name_____ Skills Assessment

VOCABULARY: Context Clues/Multiple-meaning Words

Directions: Read each passage. Fill in the answer circle in front of the correct answer for each question.

Did you know you eat sodium every day? Sodium is a mineral that occurs naturally in some foods and is often added to foods and beverages for taste. For example, sodium is added to most canned vegetables, sauces, soups, and salad dressings. Most of the sodium in our diets comes from table salt, which contains quite a bit of sodium. Our bodies need sodium, but not very much. In fact, most Americans consume too much sodium. Most of us need only a minute amount of sodium each day. It is needed to help us maintain normal blood volume and blood pressure.

13. The word table in this passage means _____.
    - Ⓐ having to do with food
    - Ⓑ to put something aside until later
    - Ⓒ a chart for showing data
    - Ⓓ the level of underground water

14. The word consume in this passage means _____.
    - Ⓐ to take up one's attention
    - Ⓑ to eat or drink
    - Ⓒ to spend
    - Ⓓ to destroy

15. The word minute in this passage means _____.
    - Ⓐ part of an hour
    - Ⓑ a dance
    - Ⓒ very small
    - Ⓓ not important

16. The word maintain in this passage means _____.
    - Ⓐ to keep in good condition
    - Ⓑ to insist something is true
    - Ⓒ to pay expenses for something
    - Ⓓ to repair something

GO ON   3

Name_____ Skills Assessment

VOCABULARY: Context Clues/Multiple-meaning Words (continued)

France is not the only country in which French is spoken. Canada, just north of the United States, has many French-speaking citizens as well. In fact, French is one of Canada's two official languages. The other official language of Canada is English. The Canadian province Quebec has the largest French-speaking population of North America. A majority of the citizens of Quebec are native speakers of French. Quebec has even passed laws to give French a privileged status, in an effort to preserve Quebec's distinct culture and heritage.

17. The word official in this passage means _____.
    - Ⓐ a police officer
    - Ⓑ an umpire or referee
    - Ⓒ recognized or authorized
    - Ⓓ not fake

18. The word native in this passage means _____.
    - Ⓐ belonging to a person's place of birth
    - Ⓑ plants grown in an area
    - Ⓒ natural or normal
    - Ⓓ dating from the distant past

19. The word passed in this passage means _____.
    - Ⓐ to make into law
    - Ⓑ to ignore
    - Ⓒ to go beyond
    - Ⓓ a ticket of admission

20. The word preserve in this passage means _____.
    - Ⓐ fruit cooked to make jelly
    - Ⓑ to keep food from spoiling
    - Ⓒ an area for wildlife
    - Ⓓ to protect or continue

4   STOP!

Name_____ **Skills Assessment**

COMPREHENSION: Compare and Contrast

Directions: Read the passage. Fill in the answer circle in front of the correct answer for each question.

Mars, the fourth planet from the sun, is on the other side of the earth from Venus. It has a cratered surface marked with canyons and ancient volcanoes. Mars has two moons named Phobos and Deimos. Venus, the third planet from the sun, has no moons. Venus is slightly smaller than Earth and covered by dense clouds. The planet with the most moons is Saturn. It has more than 20 moons. Saturn is the second largest planet and is the sixth planet from the sun. Jupiter is the largest planet. It is larger than all the other planets combined. Jupiter has sixteen known moons, two of which are larger than the planet Mercury, the planet closest to the sun.

21. According to the passage, Saturn and Mars are alike in that they both have _____ .

   Ⓐ moons
   Ⓑ dense clouds
   Ⓒ craters
   Ⓓ rings

22. Compared to Venus, Saturn _____ .

   Ⓐ has fewer moons
   Ⓑ is smaller
   Ⓒ is further from the sun
   Ⓓ is cloudier

23. Jupiter is different from all of the other planets, because it _____ .

   Ⓐ is the largest
   Ⓑ has the most moons
   Ⓒ has ancient volcanoes
   Ⓓ is closest to the sun

24. One way in which Jupiter and Saturn are alike is that they both _____ .

   Ⓐ have the same number of moons
   Ⓑ are smaller than Venus
   Ⓒ are larger than Earth
   Ⓓ are closer to the sun than Mercury

STOP!   5

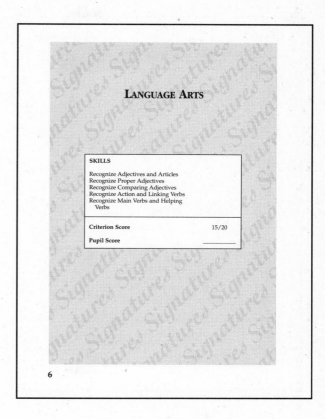

LANGUAGE ARTS

SKILLS

Recognize Adjectives and Articles
Recognize Proper Adjectives
Recognize Comparing Adjectives
Recognize Action and Linking Verbs
Recognize Main Verbs and Helping
   Verbs

Criterion Score	15/20
Pupil Score	_____

6

Sample Multiple-Choice Questions:

The first kind of question is multiple choice. Carefully read the directions and the question. Then fill in the answer circle beside the choice you think is best. Question 1 has been answered for you. Look at it and then answer question 2.

Directions: Choose the **complete subject** of each sentence.

1. Tom ran to school.
   Ⓐ Tom
   Ⓑ ran

2. The cat slept on the chair.
   Ⓐ The cat
   Ⓑ slept on the chair

Sample Write-in-the-Answer Questions:

For the second kind of question, carefully read the directions and the question. Then write your answer on the line. Question 3 has been answered for you. Look at it and then answer question 4.

Directions: Write the **complete predicate** of each sentence.

3. We went to the ball game.

   went to the ball game

4. The game was exciting.

   was exciting

7

Name_____ **Skills Assessment**

Directions: Choose the **article** in this sentence. Fill in the answer circle beside the one you choose.

1. I brought a new green wool sweater.
   Ⓐ a
   Ⓑ new
   Ⓒ green

Directions: Choose the **adjective** in this sentence. Fill in the answer circle beside the one you choose.

2. Parrots can be noisy pets that disturb the neighbors.
   Ⓐ Parrots
   Ⓑ noisy
   Ⓒ pets

Directions: Write the two **adjectives** in each sentence.

3. You can see that the black shoes won't fit her tiny feet.

   black, tiny

4. The unpaved street is filled with many potholes.

   unpaved, many

8   **GO ON**

VOCABULARY: Key Words (continued)

Directions: Choose the word that is the **proper adjective** in each sentence. Fill in the answer circle beside the one you choose.

5. My Canadian pen pal lives in a house near Montreal.

  Ⓐ Canadian
  Ⓑ pen pal
  Ⓒ Montreal

6. Her family comes from Russia and her great-grandfather was born in Poland, but she has mostly French neighbors.

  Ⓐ Russia
  Ⓑ Poland
  Ⓒ French

Directions: Write the two **proper adjectives** in this sentence.

7. Japanese rice cakes taste good with Chinese tea.

  Japanese, Chinese

Directions: Rewrite this sentence to correct the **capitalization.**

8. We ate italian sausage and spanish rice.

  We ate Italian sausage and Spanish rice.

GO ON   9

Directions: Choose the correct form of the **adjective** to go in each blank. Fill in the answer circle beside the one you choose.

9. It was the _____ day Goldilocks had ever had.

  Ⓐ bad
  Ⓑ worse
  Ⓒ worst

10. This bowl of porridge is _____ than that one.

  Ⓐ warm
  Ⓑ warmer
  Ⓒ warmest

11. Papa Bear's chair was the _____ of the three chairs.

  Ⓐ comfortable
  Ⓑ more comfortable
  Ⓒ most comfortable

12. Gino was young, but his brother Joseph was even _____ .

  Ⓐ young
  Ⓑ younger
  Ⓒ youngest

10   GO ON

Directions: Choose the **linking verb** in each sentence. Fill in the answer circle beside the one you choose.

13. This is the last day of the week.

  Ⓐ is
  Ⓑ week
  Ⓒ last

14. Insects are cold-blooded animals.

  Ⓐ are
  Ⓑ slow
  Ⓒ falls

Directions: Choose the **action verb** in this compound sentence. Fill in the answer circle beside the one you choose.

15. After his tenth birthday, Zane's family moved.

  Ⓐ after
  Ⓑ moved

Directions: Write the **action verb** in this sentence.

16. The chirps of a snowy tree cricket indicate the temperature.

  indicate

GO ON   11

Directions: Decide whether the underlined word in each sentence is a **helping verb** or a **main verb.** Fill in the answer circle beside the one you choose.

17. I will finish my homework after supper.

  Ⓐ helping verb
  Ⓑ main verb

18. Should Charlie bring your notebook?

  Ⓐ helping verb
  Ⓑ main verb

Directions: Write the **helping verb** in this sentence.

19. That elephant does walk a little faster than the others.

  does

Directions: Write the **main verb** in this sentence.

20. My children have always brought me flowers.

  brought

12   STOP!

COAST TO COAST / THEME 5

Harcourt Brace School Publishers • Skills Assessment

Name_____ Skills Assessment

DECODING: Structural Analysis

Directions: Read each sentence. Fill in the answer circle in front of the word that best completes each sentence.

1. I was not at all _____ with your sloppy work.
   - Ⓐ satisfactory
   - Ⓑ satisfied
   - Ⓒ dissatisfaction
   - Ⓓ dissatisfied

2. Molly becomes very _____ when someone criticizes her.
   - Ⓐ defend
   - Ⓑ defended
   - Ⓒ defensive
   - Ⓓ defensible

3. Roger noticed that flowers _____ bees.
   - Ⓐ attract
   - Ⓑ attraction
   - Ⓒ attractive
   - Ⓓ unattractive

4. The coach tries to _____ negative thinking.
   - Ⓐ courage
   - Ⓑ discourage
   - Ⓒ encouragement
   - Ⓓ discouragement

GO ON   1

Name_____ Skills Assessment

DECODING: Structural Analysis (continued)

5. My sister was lucky to find _____ with an excellent company.
   - Ⓐ employ
   - Ⓑ employer
   - Ⓒ employee
   - Ⓓ employment

6. When Tammy feels sluggish, she tries to _____ herself by eating a healthful snack.
   - Ⓐ energetic
   - Ⓑ energize
   - Ⓒ energy
   - Ⓓ energizer

7. We had _____ problems with that old car.
   - Ⓐ discontinue
   - Ⓑ continue
   - Ⓒ continually
   - Ⓓ continuous

8. I have a _____ that something is missing.
   - Ⓐ suspect
   - Ⓑ suspicion
   - Ⓒ suspense
   - Ⓓ suspicious

2   STOP!

Name_____ Skills Assessment

VOCABULARY: Key Words

Directions: Read each sentence. Fill in the answer circle in front of the word that best completes each sentence.

9. Eric decided to _____ his vacation day to help paint his neighbor's house.
   - Ⓐ kindness
   - Ⓑ sacrifice
   - Ⓒ determine
   - Ⓓ occupy

10. The people _____ the day on which their town was founded.
    - Ⓐ stunned
    - Ⓑ composed
    - Ⓒ endangered
    - Ⓓ commemorated

11. After the _____, the park was a clean, safe place again.
    - Ⓐ commercial
    - Ⓑ orderly
    - Ⓒ restoration
    - Ⓓ rhythm

12. The _____ of books to students takes place during the first week of school.
    - Ⓐ distribution
    - Ⓑ tradition
    - Ⓒ exhibition
    - Ⓓ culture

13. Many animals _____ these woods.
    - Ⓐ breed
    - Ⓑ provide
    - Ⓒ inhabit
    - Ⓓ observe

14. The new factory had a big _____ on the town.
    - Ⓐ stimulate
    - Ⓑ dignity
    - Ⓒ impact
    - Ⓓ satisfaction

GO ON   3

Name_____ Skills Assessment

VOCABULARY: Key Words (continued)

15. The _____ old building was going to be torn down.
    - Ⓐ desolate
    - Ⓑ indifferent
    - Ⓒ despair
    - Ⓓ inspiration

16. The only kind of meat Jack will eat is _____.
    - Ⓐ herbs
    - Ⓑ prospecting
    - Ⓒ poultry
    - Ⓓ nectar

17. I have trouble understanding the _____ spoken in that region.
    - Ⓐ detection
    - Ⓑ dialect
    - Ⓒ observation
    - Ⓓ cycle

18. We will not _____ littering in our community.
    - Ⓐ tolerate
    - Ⓑ monitor
    - Ⓒ offensive
    - Ⓓ officially

19. The Egyptian pyramids _____ the memory of the pharaohs.
    - Ⓐ decipher
    - Ⓑ necessitate
    - Ⓒ excuse
    - Ⓓ perpetuate

20. Jill always _____ the importance of being careful and taking precautions.
    - Ⓐ estimates
    - Ⓑ annoys
    - Ⓒ pressures
    - Ⓓ emphasizes

4   STOP!

COMPREHENSION: Main Idea and Details

Directions: Read the passage. Fill in the answer circle in front of the correct answer for each question.

Winter, spring, summer, fall. The four seasons come and go, but have you ever wondered *why* we have seasons? Contrary to what some people believe, our seasons are not caused by the fact that the Earth's orbit around the Sun is an ellipse—an oval shape. Instead, the seasons are caused by the tilt of the Earth's axis. The Earth's axis is an imaginary line that goes through the center of the Earth, beginning at the North Pole and ending at the South Pole. When the northern end of the Earth's axis tilts away from the Sun, the southern axis is tilting toward the Sun. That makes it colder in the northern hemisphere, so you have winter. At the same time, it is warmer in the southern hemisphere, so people there have summer.

21. What is the main idea of this passage?

Ⓐ Summer is a season.
Ⓑ We do not understand what causes our seasons.
Ⓒ Seasons are caused by the tilt of Earth's axis.
Ⓓ People live in the northern hemisphere.

22. Which of the following details best supports the main idea?

Ⓐ The Earth's axis is an imaginary line.
Ⓑ The seasons come and go.
Ⓒ The Earth's orbit is an ellipse.
Ⓓ The northern axis tilts away from the Sun during winter.

23. It is winter in the southern hemisphere when _____ .

Ⓐ the southern axis tilts away from the Sun
Ⓑ the southern axis tilts toward the Sun
Ⓒ the northern axis tilts away from the Sun
Ⓓ Earth's axis is not tilted

24. When it is winter in the northern hemisphere, what season is it in the southern hemisphere?

Ⓐ winter
Ⓑ spring
Ⓒ summer
Ⓓ fall

STOP! 5

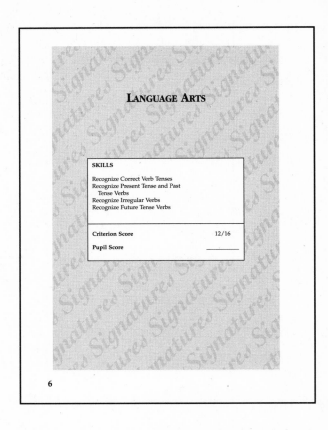

LANGUAGE ARTS

SKILLS

Recognize Correct Verb Tenses
Recognize Present Tense and Past Tense Verbs
Recognize Irregular Verbs
Recognize Future Tense Verbs

Criterion Score	12/16
Pupil Score	_____

6

Sample Multiple-Choice Questions:

The first kind of question is multiple choice. Carefully read the directions and the question. Then fill in the answer circle beside the choice you think is best. Question 1 has been answered for you. Look at it and then answer question 2.

Directions: Choose the **complete subject** of each sentence.

1. Tom ran to school.
   Ⓐ Tom
   Ⓑ ran

2. The cat slept on the chair.
   Ⓐ The cat
   Ⓑ slept on the chair

Sample Write-in-the-Answer Questions:

For the second kind of question, carefully read the directions and the question. Then write your answer on the line. Question 3 has been answered for you. Look at it and then answer question 4.

Directions: Write the **complete predicate** of each sentence.

3. We went to the ball game.
   went to the ball game

4. The game was exciting.
   was exciting

7

Directions: Decide whether each sentence is in the **past, present,** or **future tense.** Fill in the answer circle beside the one you choose.

1. You will find many interesting seaweeds on the beach.
   Ⓐ past tense
   Ⓑ present tense
   Ⓒ future tense

2. Look for the sea oak, which resembles a red oak leaf.
   Ⓐ past tense
   Ⓑ present tense
   Ⓒ future tense

3. Sea oaks grow on other seaweeds, such as kelp.
   Ⓐ past tense
   Ⓑ present tense
   Ⓒ future tense

Directions: Write the two **verbs** in this sentence that are in the **past tense.**

4. My friend Shantelle cooked some kelp, and I tasted it.
   cooked, tasted _____

8 **GO ON**

Directions: Choose the correct form of the **verb** to complete each sentence. Fill in the answer circle beside the one you choose.

5. The lumber was _____ in a drying room, called a kiln.

Ⓐ dries
Ⓑ dried
Ⓒ dry

6. Mark has _____ many mistakes in this article.

Ⓐ find
Ⓑ found
Ⓒ finding

Directions: Choose the **present tense** of the verb to complete the sentence.

7. Jonelle _____ up her paintings.

Ⓐ box
Ⓑ boxes
Ⓒ boxing

Directions: Write the **past tense** of the underlined **verb**.

8. Gail went right outside and call them.

called

GO ON   9

Directions: Write the **present tense** of the underlined **verb**.

9. Everyone wish on a star at least once in a lifetime.

wishes

Directions: Choose the **irregular verb** in this compound sentence. Fill in the answer circle beside the one you choose.

10. Geo and Liz carry the food, we bring the lawn chairs, and Hosea and his brother help with the drinks.

Ⓐ carry
Ⓑ bring
Ⓒ help

Directions: Write the **past-tense** of the verb in this sentence.

11. We never stand still!

stood

Directions: Rewrite this sentence to correct the underlined **verbs**.

12. Sit the alarm clock on the table before you lay down.

Set the alarm clock on the table before you lie down.

10   GO ON

Directions: Choose whether the underlined **verb** shows a **past, future,** or **present action.** Fill in the answer circle beside the one you choose.

13. Lily will participate in the Special Olympics this year.

Ⓐ past action
Ⓑ future action
Ⓒ present action

Directions: Choose the **future tense** of the verb in this sentence. Fill in the answer circle beside the one you choose.

14. My family will never move to a cold climate.

Ⓐ will move
Ⓑ never move
Ⓒ move to

Directions: Rewrite each sentence so the verb is in the **future tense.**

15. Mary is writing to her parents.

Mary will write to her parents.

16. Ken hits the puck into the net!

Ken will hit the puck into the net!

STOP!   11

Harcourt Brace School Publishers • Skills Assessment

COAST TO COAST / THEME 6

VOCABULARY: Key Words

Directions: Read each sentence. Fill in the answer circle in front of the word that best completes each sentence.

1. We elected him to be our _____ in Washington.

Ⓐ patient   Ⓑ impression
Ⓒ confident   Ⓓ spokesperson

2. The boy did not have _____ training in music.

Ⓐ partial   Ⓑ culture
Ⓒ formal   Ⓓ reliable

3. Wearing a uniform is _____ in some schools.

Ⓐ compulsory   Ⓑ reluctant
Ⓒ irritated   Ⓓ minimal

4. The job pays $200 a week plus free _____ .

Ⓐ assault and battery   Ⓑ room and board
Ⓒ determination   Ⓓ occupation

5. Paula came up with the _____ idea that saved the day.

Ⓐ ingenious   Ⓑ heroine
Ⓒ cautiously   Ⓓ many

6. We saw several _____ fields among the wood lots.

Ⓐ chanting   Ⓑ legendary
Ⓒ rustle   Ⓓ cultivated

GO ON   1

VOCABULARY: Key Words (continued)

7. My parents attempted to _____ my confidence before I performed on stage.

(A) bolster   (B) emerge
(C) counter   (D) grant

8. We are _____ to know how our tax dollars are spent.

(A) conscious   (B) dreaded
(C) entitled   (D) stunning

9. This organization was _____ in 1942.

(A) founded   (B) improvised
(C) indicated   (D) lower

10. This painting is my greatest _____ .

(A) eagerly   (B) audition
(C) accomplishment   (D) succeed

11. The _____ soldiers traveled on foot, while horses carried the wounded.

(A) victim   (B) able-bodied
(C) well-respected   (D) artificial

12. We discussed the _____ of the new rules.

(A) superiors   (B) ebb and flow
(C) pros and cons   (D) satisfaction

Coast to Coast • Skills Assessment • Harcourt Brace School Publishers

2   **GO ON**

VOCABULARY: Key Words (continued)

13. The _____ of the town voted for a new mayor.

(A) citizens   (B) heritage
(C) hostility   (D) locale

14. My _____ came to the United States from Europe.

(A) dexterity   (B) ancestors
(C) colony   (D) dignity

15. There were no stores in the _____ neighborhood.

(A) residential   (B) commercial
(C) symmetrical   (D) chronic

16. She runs a _____ company that has grown every year.

(A) translated   (B) prosperous
(C) deserted   (D) stagnant

Coast to Coast • Skills Assessment • Harcourt Brace School Publishers

STOP!   **3**

COMPREHENSION: Summarize/Paraphrase

Directions: Read each passage. Fill in the answer circle in front of the correct answer for each question.

Denise was excited when her teacher announced that her class would put on a production of *The Wizard of Oz*. Denise announced that she'd like to be the cowardly lion.

"You can't be the cowardly lion!" Jerry protested. "The cowardly lion is a boy, and you're a girl."

"What difference does it make?" Denise replied. "If I can play the role well, then it shouldn't make any difference."

Denise's teacher agreed. "Denise can try out for the part. The play is a fantasy story anyway. If Denise can learn the lines and play the part, it doesn't matter whether the character is played by a girl or a boy. What's more important is that we all work hard and have fun."

Once that was settled, tryouts began and they proceeded to cast the play.

17. Which of the following statements best summarizes this passage?

(A) Denise is someone who always gets her way.
(B) Denise's class decided to put on a production of *The Wizard of Oz*.
(C) In this fantasy play, Denise can try out for the role of the cowardly lion.
(D) Boys and girls rarely agree on anything.

18. What is another way of saying "They proceeded to cast the play."

(A) They began to assign character roles to people.
(B) They began to practice presenting the play.
(C) They threw out the idea of presenting the play.
(D) They had a party for everyone in the play.

4   **GO ON**

COMPREHENSION: Summarize/Paraphrase (continued)

Colin will never forget the advice his dad gave him when he was a young man. Colin was getting ready to leave for college the fall after he had graduated from high school. He was a little nervous about leaving home and going out on his own. Although he had never gone to college himself, Colin's dad was a very wise man. He said, "Colin, you must always follow your dreams, for dreams are the most important things we have. They motivate us to keep going. They give us hope. Don't ever lose sight of your dreams, Colin." Colin still remembers these words although they were spoken to him many years ago. Colin followed his father's advice and, after graduating from college, he lived and worked overseas for a number of years.

19. Which of the following statements best summarizes this passage?

(A) Colin graduated from high school many years ago.
(B) Colin's father has not spoken to him in many years.
(C) Colin remembered and followed his father's advice.
(D) All of Colin's dreams came true because his father helped him.

20. What is another way of saying, "Always follow your dreams"?

(A) Don't let your dreams get in your way.
(B) Ideas will come to you in your sleep.
(C) Try to achieve your goals in life.
(D) Keep on daydreaming.

Harcourt Brace School Publishers • Skills Assessment

GO ON   **5**

COMPREHENSION: Summarize/Paraphrase (continued)

Darla was home with the flu. It was not where she wanted to be. She could picture her friends in school going to classes, eating lunch, and playing in the schoolyard. No one likes being ill, but Darla was trying to make the best of it. She read a book, worked on a crossword puzzle, and listened to the radio. She also drank lots of juice. The doctor had said she could go back to school after her temperature was normal for 24 hours. Darla knew she would feel better soon. In the meantime she just had to take care of herself.

21. Which of the following statements best summarizes this passage?

(A) Darla likes to read.
(B) Darla must drink lots of juice.
(C) Darla's doctor took her temperature.
(D) Darla is recovering from the flu.

22. What is another way of saying, "Darla was trying to make the best of it"?

(A) Darla was trying to enjoy what she could.
(B) Darla was doing a big project.
(C) Darla always wanted to be better than others.
(D) Darla could hardly wait to get better.

6   **GO ON**

COMPREHENSION: Summarize/Paraphrase (continued)

Wendy awoke in the middle of the night, realizing that something was wrong. She glanced over at her clock. Two o'clock in the morning. What had waked her up? She smelled the smoke at the same instant she saw the flames outside her window. Wendy scrambled to the door but felt it carefully before she opened it, as she had been taught to do. The door was not hot, so Wendy knew it was safe to open it.

By the time Wendy opened the front door, her mother was already outside drenching the flames with a garden hose, and her father was standing by with a shovel. They never discovered what caused the pile of dry leaves to burn, but they were all glad the fire had been detected and put out before any harm was done.

23. Which of the following statements best summarizes the passage?

(A) Wendy was injured in a fire.
(B) Wendy's parents put out a fire.
(C) Wendy was having a dream about a fire.
(D) Wendy's family figured out how the fire started.

24. What is another way of saying, "Her father was standing by with a shovel"?

(A) Her father was standing very close to a shovel.
(B) Her father took a shovel and walked away with it.
(C) Her father was digging a hole with a shovel.
(D) Her father was standing in a store where he went to buy a new shovel.

STOP!   7

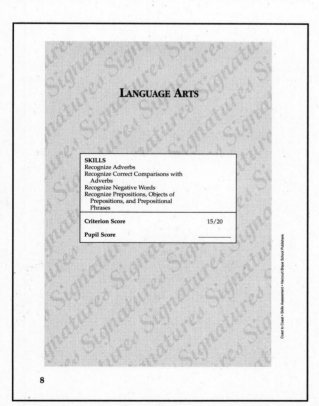

LANGUAGE ARTS

SKILLS
Recognize Adverbs
Recognize Correct Comparisons with
   Adverbs
Recognize Negative Words
Recognize Prepositions, Objects of
   Prepositions, and Prepositional
   Phrases

Criterion Score	15/20
Pupil Score	_____

8

Sample Multiple-Choice Questions:

The first kind of question is multiple choice. Carefully read the directions and the question. Then fill in the answer circle beside the choice you think is best. Question 1 has been answered for you. Look at it and then answer question 2.

Directions: Choose the **complete subject** of each sentence.

1. Tom ran to school.
(A) Tom
(B) ran

2. The cat slept on the chair.
(A) The cat
(B) slept on the chair

Sample Write-in-the-Answer Questions:

For the second kind of question, carefully read the directions and the question. Then write your answer on the line. Question 3 has been answered for you. Look at it and then answer question 4.

Directions: Write the **complete predicate** of each sentence.

3. We went to the ball game.
   went to the ball game

4. The game was exciting.
   was exciting

9

Directions: Choose the **adverb** in each sentence. Fill in the answer circle beside the one you choose.

1. Stay away from angrily snarling dogs and busy mothers.
   - (A) stay
   - (B) angrily
   - (C) snarling

2. Theodore Roosevelt said, "Speak softly and carry a big stick."
   - (A) softly
   - (B) carry
   - (C) big

Directions: Write the two **adverbs** in each sentence.

3. He had forty-two boxes, all carefully packed, with his name printed clearly on each.
   carefully, clearly

4. The jury almost always took notes.
   almost always

Directions: Decide what or who is being compared by the **adverb** in this sentence. Fill in the answer circle beside the one you choose.

5. Lynn's two young dogs play harder than Jeff's old one.
   - (A) Lynn and Jeff
   - (B) Lynn's two dogs
   - (C) Lynn's dogs and Jeff's dog

Directions: Choose the correct form of the **adverb** to go in each blank. Fill in the answer circle beside the one you choose.

6. Chris clears the table _____ than his brother.
   - (A) quickly
   - (B) most quickly
   - (C) more quickly

GO ON

7. Because of the lower gravity, astronauts can jump _____ on the moon than on Earth.
   - (A) high
   - (B) higher
   - (C) highest

8. Of all the people I know, Nancy sprints _____.
   - (A) well
   - (B) best
   - (C) good

Directions: Write the **negative** word or words in each sentence.

9. I never do my homework late at night.
   never

10. He's not a very friendly dog, so nobody bothers him.
    not, nobody

Directions: Rewrite this sentence to make it correct.

11. We don't have no money.
    We have no money, or We don't have any money, or We haven't any money.

Directions: Rewrite this sentence to make it a **negative** statement.

12. This is Jenna's house.
    This isn't Jenna's house, or This house is not Jenna's.

Directions: Choose the **preposition** in each sentence. Fill in the answer circle beside the one you choose.

13. Go over the bridge and turn right.
    - (A) Go
    - (B) over
    - (C) turn

14. Heavy rains arrived after the long dry spell.
    - (A) heavy
    - (B) after
    - (C) long

GO ON

Directions: Choose the word in this sentence that is the **object of a preposition**. Fill in the answer circle beside the one you choose.

15. Alice and I walked slowly toward the city.
    - (A) Alice
    - (B) I
    - (C) city

Directions: Choose the words in this sentence that form a **prepositional phrase**. Fill in the answer circle beside the one you choose.

16. Inside the cage, green parakeets hopped and fluttered.
    - (A) Inside the cage
    - (B) green parakeets
    - (C) hopped and fluttered

Directions: Write the **preposition** in each sentence.

17. A little dog trotted by the old man's side.
    by

18. She came without a suitcase and didn't stay long.
    without

Directions: Write the **object of a preposition** in this sentence.

19. He received a letter from his friend.
    friend

Directions: Write the words from this rhyme that form **a prepositional phrase**.

20. "I said it very loud and clear; I went and shouted in his ear."
    in his ear

STOP!

Harcourt Brace School Publishers • Skills Assessment

ANSWER KEY SKILLS ASSESSMENT: READING
GRADE 5: COAST TO COAST

THEME 1	THEME 2	THEME 3	THEME 4	THEME 5	THEME 6
Vocabulary (Key Words)	**Vocabulary (Key Words)**	**Vocabulary (Key Words)**	**Vocabulary (Key Words)**	**Decoding (Structural Analysis)**	**Vocabulary (Key Words)**
1. D	1. B	1. D	1. D	1. B	1. D
2. A	2. C	2. B	2. B	2. C	2. C
3. C	3. A	3. A	3. A	3. A	3. A
4. A	4. B	4. D	4. D	4. B	4. B
5. B	5. A	5. A	5. C	5. D	5. A
6. D	6. A	6. C	6. A	6. B	6. D
7. C	7. D	7. B	7. C	7. D	7. A
8. A	8. C	8. D	8. B	8. B	8. C
9. B	9. B	9. D	9. A		9. A
10. A	10. D	10. A	10. C	**Vocabulary (Key Words)**	10. C
11. D	11. A	11. D	11. C	9. B	11. B
12. A	12. D	12. C	12. B	10. D	12. C
13. C				11. C	13. A
14. C	**Comprehension (Make Predictions/ Draw Conclusions)**	**Literary Appreciation (Narrative Elements)**	**(Context Clues/ Multiple Meaning Words)**	12. A	14. B
15. A				13. C	15. A
16. D				14. C	16. B
	13. C	13. B	13. A	15. A	
Comprehension (Sequence/ Cause and Effect)	14. D	14. A	14. B	16. C	**Comprehension (Summarize/ Paraphrase)**
	15. D	15. D	15. C	17. B	
	16. B	16. A	16. A	18. A	17. C
17. C		17. D	17. C	19. D	18. A
18. D	**(Fact and Opinion/ Author's Purpose and Viewpoint)**	18. A	18. A	20. D	19. C
19. C		19. A	19. A		20. C
20. B		20. B	20. D	**Comprehension (Main Idea and Details)**	21. D
21. A					22. A
22. C	17. A	**Study Skills (Reference Sources)**	**Comprehension (Compare and Contrast)**	21. C	23. B
23. C	18. B			22. D	24. A
24. B	19. D	21. C	21. A	23. A	
	20. C	22. A	22. C	24. C	
	21. A	23. B	23. A		
	22. B	24. D	24. C		
	23. B				
	24. D				

Harcourt Brace School Publishers • Skills Assessment

Answer Keys Skills Assessment: Language Arts
Grade 5: Coast to Coast

Theme 1	Theme 2	Theme 3
1. B	1. B	1. A
2. A	2. A	2. A
3. C	3. were falling like snow	3. son, bottom
4. A	4. Red and white tulips	4. The robins perched on the branches.
5. B	5. A	5. C
6. D	6. B	6. children's, Chicago's
7. C	7. Swimming, sailing	7. B
8. D	8. children, friends	8. C
9. Fish	9. B	9. C
10. huddled together for warmth	10. A	10. A
11. subject	11. Ask Julie the question. She might not know the answer.	11. A
12. predicate	12. or	12. We, he, himself, them
	13. B	13. C
	14. A	14. A
	15. grandmother, home	15. him
	16. Old Faithful, Yellowstone National Park	16. We

Harcourt Brace School Publishers • Skills Assessment

Answer Keys Skills Assessment: Language Arts
Grade 5: Coast to Coast

Theme 4

1. A
2. B
3. black, tiny
4. unpaved, many
5. A
6. C
7. Japanese, Chinese
8. We ate Italian sausage and Spanish rice.
9. C
10. B
11. C
12. B
13. A
14. A
15. B
16. indicate
17. A
18. B
19. does
20. brought

Theme 5

1. C
2. B
3. B
4. cooked, tasted
5. B
6. B
7. B
8. called
9. wishes
10. B
11. stood
12. Set the alarm clock on the table before you lie down.
13. B
14. A
15. Mary will write to her parents.
16. Ken will hit the puck into the net!

Theme 6

1. B
2. A
3. carefully, clearly
4. almost, always
5. C
6. C
7. B
8. B
9. never
10. not, nobody
11. We have no money. (or) We don't have any money. (or) We haven't any money.
12. This is not Jenna's house. (or) This house is not Jenna's.
13. B
14. B
15. C
16. A
17. by
18. without
19. friend
20. in his ear

Harcourt Brace School Publishers • Skills Assessment

APPENDIX

Coping Masters

Theme 1
Skills Assessment: Reading
Skills Assessment: Language Arts

Theme 2
Skills Assessment: Reading
Skills Assessment: Language Arts

Theme 3
Skills Assessment: Reading
Skills Assessment: Language Arts

Theme 4
Skills Assessment: Reading
Skills Assessment: Language Arts

Theme 5
Skills Assessment: Reading
Skills Assessment: Language Arts

Theme 6
Skills Assessment: Reading
Skills Assessment: Language Arts

STUDENT RECORD FORM
SKILLS ASSESSMENT: READING

Signatures   **Grade 5**

Name_____ Grade_____

Teacher_____

Coast to Coast / Theme 1

	Number Possible	Criterion Score	Number Correct	Diagnostic Category
Key words	16	12		
Sequence/Cause and effect	8	6		

Coast to Coast / Theme 2

	Number Possible	Criterion Score	Number Correct	Diagnostic Category
Key words	12	9		
Make predictions/Draw conclusions	4	3		
Fact and Opinion/Author's purpose and viewpoint	8	6		

Coast to Coast / Theme 3

	Number Possible	Criterion Score	Number Correct	Diagnostic Category
Key words	12	9		
Narrative elements	8	6		
Reference sources	4	3		

Coast to Coast / Theme 4

	Number Possible	Criterion Score	Number Correct	Diagnostic Category
Key words	12	9		
Context clues /Multiple=meaning words	8	6		
Compare and contrast	4	3		

Coast to Coast / Theme 5

	Number Possible	Criterion Score	Number Correct	Diagnostic Category
Structural Analysis: Prefixes, suffixes, and roots	8	6		
Key words	12	9		
Main idea and details	4	3		

Coast to Coast / Theme 6

	Number Possible	Criterion Score	Number Correct	Diagnostic Category
Key words	16	12		
Summarize/Paraphrase	8	6		

Harcourt Brace School Publishers • Skills Assessment

STUDENT RECORD FORM
SKILLS ASSESSMENT: LANGUAGE ARTS

Signatures   Grade 5

Name_____   Grade_____

Teacher_____

Coast to Coast / Theme 1   Date_____

SKILL	SCORES
Declarative, interrogative, exclamatory, and imperative sentences Subjects and predicates	Number Possible: 12 Criterion Score: 9 Pupil Score: _____

Coast to Coast / Theme 2   Date_____

Complete and simple subjects and predicates Compound subjects and predicates Simple and compound sentences Conjunctions Common and proper nouns	Number Possible: 16 Criterion Score: 12 Pupil Score: _____

Coast to Coast / Theme 3   Date_____

Singular and plural nouns Possessive nouns Pronouns and antecedents Subject, object, reflexive, and possessive pronouns	Number Possible: 16 Criterion Score: 12 Pupil Score: _____

Student Record Form
Skills Assessment: Language Arts

Signatures   **Grade 5**

Name_____   Grade_____

Teacher_____

Coast to Coast / Theme 4   Date_____

SKILL	SCORES
Adjectives and articles Proper adjectives Comparing adjectives Action and linking verbs Main verbs and helping verbs	Number Possible: 20 Criterion Score: 15 Pupil Score: _____

Coast to Coast / Theme 5   Date_____

Correct verb tenses Past, present, and future-tense verbs Irregular verbs	Number Possible: 16 Criterion Score: 12 Pupil Score: _____

Coast to Coast / Theme 6   Date_____

Adverbs Comparing adverbs Negative words Prepositions, objects of prepositions, and prepositional phrases	Number Possible: 20 Criterion Score: 15 Pupil Score: _____

Harcourt Brace School Publishers • Skills Assessment

Skills Assessment:
Reading and Language Arts

Coast to Coast/Theme 1

Name _____ Date _____

Reading

SKILL AREA	Criterion Score	Pupil Score	Pupil Strength
VOCABULARY Key Words	12/16	_____	_____
COMPREHENSION Sequence/Cause and Effect	6/8	_____	_____
TOTAL SCORE	18/24	_____	_____

HARCOURT
BRACE

Copyright © by Harcourt Brace & Company

All rights reserved. No part of this publication may be reproduced
or transmitted in any form or by any means, electronic or mechanical, including
photocopy, recording, or any information storage and retrieval system.

Teachers using SIGNATURES may photocopy complete pages
in sufficient quantities for classroom use only and not for resale.

HARCOURT BRACE and Quill Design is a registered
trademark of Harcourt Brace & Company.

Printed in the United States of America

ISBN 0-15-308236-4

1 2 3 4 5 6 7 8 9 10 085 99 98 97 96

VOCABULARY: Key Words

Directions: Read each sentence. Fill in the answer circle in front of the word that best completes each sentence.

1. I gave my friend a _____ of my new computer game.

   Ⓐ companion   Ⓑ demolition
   Ⓒ completion   Ⓓ demonstration

2. George tried to _____ the sound of his alarm clock with his pillow.

   Ⓐ muffle   Ⓑ enhance
   Ⓒ disgrace   Ⓓ volunteer

3. The _____ divided the room.

   Ⓐ cycle   Ⓑ herb
   Ⓒ partition   Ⓓ quantity

4. My little sister _____ around my bedroom when I'm not at home.

   Ⓐ prowls   Ⓑ previews
   Ⓒ interrupts   Ⓓ denies

5. Michael prefers to write _____ instead of poetry.

   Ⓐ occupation   Ⓑ prose
   Ⓒ compose   Ⓓ current

6. I sat outside the principal's door, _____ waiting for her to call me into her office.

   Ⓐ traditionally   Ⓑ destiny
   Ⓒ afraid   Ⓓ anxiously

Coast to Coast • Skills Assessment • Harcourt Brace School Publishers

VOCABULARY: Key Words (continued)

7. Sarah tried to sound _____ when she told her friend about her part in the school play.

Ⓐ despair   Ⓑ interrupted
Ⓒ nonchalant   Ⓓ shriveled

8. _____ such as being able to watch television are earned through good behavior.

Ⓐ Privileges   Ⓑ Pledges
Ⓒ Instincts   Ⓓ Qualities

9. After I told my brother I'd lost all my money, he said _____ , "You are so responsible."

Ⓐ hostility   Ⓑ sarcastically
Ⓒ unreliable   Ⓓ noticeably

10. I will be the _____ of the fifth grade if I wear my shoes on the wrong feet again.

Ⓐ laughingstock   Ⓑ bulldozer
Ⓒ amateur   Ⓓ embarrass

11. After he robbed the bank, the _____ escaped.

Ⓐ custom   Ⓑ defiant
Ⓒ expression   Ⓓ culprit

12. Our dog was _____ at Grandma's feet, begging her to give him one more bone.

Ⓐ groveling   Ⓑ concealing
Ⓒ cautiously   Ⓓ disguising

Coast to Coast • Skills Assessment • Harcourt Brace School Publishers

GO ON

VOCABULARY: Key Words (continued)

13. I _____ every time I see a mouse.

    Ⓐ mimic   Ⓑ supply
    Ⓒ cringe   Ⓓ resemble

14. The boat's _____ was broken, so we couldn't go out on the lake.

    Ⓐ property   Ⓑ recovery
    Ⓒ propeller   Ⓓ chisel

15. When my cousin had _____ , he was in the hospital.

    Ⓐ pneumonia   Ⓑ scientist
    Ⓒ javelin   Ⓓ neutral

16. Amanda was so _____ she could barely speak.

    Ⓐ coiled   Ⓑ jubilation
    Ⓒ offhanded   Ⓓ flustered

Coast to Coast • Skills Assessment • Harcourt Brace School Publishers

COMPREHENSION: Sequence/Cause and Effect

> **Directions:** Read each passage. Fill in the answer circle in front of the correct answer for each question.

Heather and her mother decided to bake cookies. First, they made a list of ingredients they needed and then drove to the store. When they got home, to save time, Heather preheated the oven while her mother placed things on the counter. Then, Heather measured and mixed dry ingredients while her mom greased the cookie sheets. Next, Heather cracked eggs into a separate bowl and added all the remaining ingredients. She mixed half the ingredients with a blender. Slowly, Heather added the dry ingredients to the egg mixture. Finally, it was time to add the chocolate chips. Then, Heather dropped balls of dough onto a cookie sheet and put it in the oven. The smell of baking cookies drew Heather's father into the kitchen. A few minutes later, they all ate freshly baked cookies and drank milk.

17. Why did Heather and her mother make a list before going to the store?
    - (A) They wanted to bake cookies.
    - (B) Heather wanted chocolate chips.
    - (C) To make sure they had all the ingredients.
    - (D) They were out of milk.

18. While Heather preheated the oven, her mother _____ .
    - (A) called her father to the kitchen
    - (B) cracked the eggs
    - (C) dropped balls of dough onto a cookie sheet
    - (D) placed things on the counter

19. Heather added the chocolate chips before _____ .
    - (A) she preheated the oven
    - (B) her mom greased the cookie sheets
    - (C) her father came into the kitchen
    - (D) she used the blender

20. Why did Heather's father come into the kitchen?
    - (A) He wanted to talk to Heather.
    - (B) He smelled baking cookies.
    - (C) Heather called him.
    - (D) He wanted to bake cookies.

Coast to Coast • Skills Assessment • Harcourt Brace School Publishers

GO ON

COMPREHENSION: Sequence/Cause and Effect (continued)

David's mom asked him to go to the grocery store after school to buy bread, potatoes, lettuce, and cheese.

"Make a list so you won't forget anything," she suggested.

"Don't worry, Mom. I'll remember," David replied.

David went to the grocery store. He bought the potatoes, lettuce, and cheese and then went home. That's when David realized he should have made a list after all. He'd have to go back to the store for the bread.

21. When did David go to the store?

   Ⓐ after school
   Ⓑ before he went to school
   Ⓒ when his homework was done
   Ⓓ after he did his chores around the house

22. Why couldn't David's mother make him a cheese sandwich when he got home?

   Ⓐ She thought it would spoil his dinner.
   Ⓑ She was out of cheese.
   Ⓒ She was out of bread.
   Ⓓ He wasn't hungry.

Coast to Coast • Skills Assessment • Harcourt Brace School Publishers

COMPREHENSION: Sequence/Cause and Effect (continued)

Eric was surprised when his older sister Nina invited him to go to a movie with her and her friends. Eric was nervous and excited about going to a movie with the older kids. While he was getting ready, he decided he didn't like the pants he was wearing, so he changed into a new pair.

At the movie theater, Eric reached for his wallet, but it wasn't there. "Oh, no," he thought. "What happened to my wallet? Where could it be?"

Just then Nina said, "Eric, I'm glad you could come with us. I never did thank you properly for helping me clean the family room for my party, so I'd like to pay for your movie ticket."

23. Because Eric helped Nina clean the family room, _____ .

    Ⓐ Nina bought Eric a new pair of pants
    Ⓑ Nina helped Eric paint his room
    Ⓒ Nina treated Eric to a movie
    Ⓓ Nina gave a party for Eric

24. When did Eric realize he didn't have his wallet with him?
    Ⓐ When he was thinking about going to the movies.
    Ⓑ After he got to the movie theater.
    Ⓒ When his sister paid for his ticket.
    Ⓓ When he changed into a new pair of pants.

STOP!

Coast to Coast • Skills Assessment • Harcourt Brace School Publishers

LANGUAGE ARTS

SKILLS

Recognize Declarative, Interrogative,
Exclamatory, and Imperative
Sentences
Recognize Subjects and Predicates

Criterion Score	9/12
Pupil Score	_____

Sample Multiple-Choice Questions:

The first kind of question is multiple choice. Carefully read the directions and the question. Then fill in the answer circle beside the choice you think is best. Question 1 has been answered for you. Look at it and then answer question 2.

Directions: Choose the **complete subject** of each sentence.

1.　Tom ran to school.

　　Ⓐ Tom
　　Ⓑ ran

2.　The cat slept on the chair.

　　Ⓐ The cat
　　Ⓑ slept on the chair

Sample Write-in-the-Answer Questions:

For the second kind of question, carefully read the directions and the question. Then write your answer on the line. Question 3 has been answered for you. Look at it and then answer question 4.

Directions: Write the **complete predicate** of each sentence.

3.　We went to the ball game.

　　went to the ball game　　　　　　　　　

4.　The game was exciting.

Coast to Coast • Skills Assessment • Harcourt Brace School Publishers

Directions: Decide whether each sentence is **declarative, interrogative, exclamatory,** or **imperative.** Fill in the answer circle beside the one you choose.

1. Who ate the last piece of chocolate cake?

    Ⓐ declarative
    Ⓑ interrogative
    Ⓒ exclamatory
    Ⓓ imperative

2. I didn't even get a piece of cake.

    Ⓐ declarative
    Ⓑ interrogative
    Ⓒ exclamatory
    Ⓓ imperative

3. I didn't take it!

    Ⓐ declarative
    Ⓑ interrogative
    Ⓒ exclamatory
    Ⓓ imperative

4. Mom bought the cake Monday morning.

    Ⓐ declarative
    Ⓑ interrogative
    Ⓒ exclamatory
    Ⓓ imperative

GO ON

Coast to Coast • Skills Assessment • Harcourt Brace School Publishers

5. What did your teacher tell you?

    Ⓐ declarative
    Ⓑ interrogative
    Ⓒ exclamatory
    Ⓓ imperative

6. Don't drop that box.

    Ⓐ declarative
    Ⓑ interrogative
    Ⓒ exclamatory
    Ⓓ imperative

7. How cold that water is!

    Ⓐ declarative
    Ⓑ interrogative
    Ⓒ exclamatory
    Ⓓ imperative

8. Pass me the scissors.

    Ⓐ declarative
    Ⓑ interrogative
    Ⓒ exclamatory
    Ⓓ imperative

Coast to Coast • Skills Assessment • Harcourt Brace School Publishers

Directions: Write the **subject** of this sentence.

9. Fish darted in and out of the shallows.

_____

Directions: Write the complete **predicate** of this sentence.

10. The chickens huddled together for warmth.

_____

Directions: Tell whether the **subject** or the **predicate** is missing from each sentence.

11. Was going to get his way, no matter what.

_____

12. Tommy and the guys from his baseball team.

_____

Coast to Coast • Skills Assessment • Harcourt Brace School Publishers

Signatures

COAST TO COAST

SKILLS ASSESSMENT

IN AND OUT OF SCHOOL/THEME 1

HARCOURT
BRACE

ORLANDO ATLANTA AUSTIN BOSTON SAN FRANCISCO CHICAGO DALLAS NEW YORK
TORONTO LONDON

PART NO. 9997-17411-9

ISBN 0-15-308236-4   (PACKAGE OF 12)

5

Skills Assessment: Reading and Language Arts

Coast to Coast/Theme 2

Name _____   Date _____

Reading

SKILL AREA	Criterion Score	Pupil Score	Pupil Strength
VOCABULARY Key Words	9/12	_____	_____
COMPREHENSION Make Predictions/ Draw Conclusions	3/4	_____	_____
Fact and Opinion/Author's Purpose and Viewpoint	6/8	_____	_____
TOTAL SCORE	18/24	_____	_____

HARCOURT BRACE

Copyright © by Harcourt Brace & Company

All rights reserved. No part of this publication may be reproduced
or transmitted in any form or by any means, electronic or mechanical, including
photocopy, recording, or any information storage and retrieval system.

Teachers using SIGNATURES may photocopy complete pages
in sufficient quantities for classroom use only and not for resale.

HARCOURT BRACE and Quill Design is a registered
trademark of Harcourt Brace & Company.

Printed in the United States of America

ISBN 0-15-308236-4

1 2 3 4 5 6 7 8 9 10   085   99 98 97 96

VOCABULARY: Key Words

Directions: Read each sentence. Fill in the answer circle in front of the word that best completes each sentence.

1. When I get home from school, I like to relax in my _____ .

   Ⓐ heritage   Ⓑ hammock
   Ⓒ current   Ⓓ exhibit

2. Since no one paid attention to me, I felt as though I were _____ .

   Ⓐ conscious   Ⓑ recovery
   Ⓒ invisible   Ⓓ mechanical

3. Receiving a phone call from my favorite uncle made my birthday very _____.

   Ⓐ memorable   Ⓑ impatient
   Ⓒ celebration   Ⓓ indifferent

4. The weary _____ came ashore after months at sea.

   Ⓐ mergers   Ⓑ mariners
   Ⓒ frontiers   Ⓓ expressions

5. The _____ for our trip were put on the boat before we left.

   Ⓐ provisions   Ⓑ festivities
   Ⓒ splendid   Ⓓ inspiration

6. The principal _____ the school's new flag for all to see.

   Ⓐ unfurled   Ⓑ rebuilt
   Ⓒ emerges   Ⓓ ignored

Coast to Coast • Skills Assessment • Harcourt Brace School Publishers

VOCABULARY: Key Words (continued)

7. The _____ cheered their team to victory.

   Ⓐ surroundings   Ⓑ determination
   Ⓒ sleighs   Ⓓ spectators

8. The teacher _____ the students' request to hold class outdoors.

   Ⓐ illustrated   Ⓑ convinced
   Ⓒ vetoed   Ⓓ transmits

9. She has the _____ to make many of her own decisions.

   Ⓐ loyalty   Ⓑ liberty
   Ⓒ independent   Ⓓ oppression

10. My uncle's apple trees _____ a huge crop each year.

   Ⓐ descend   Ⓑ quantity
   Ⓒ compose   Ⓓ yield

11. Caroline consulted two _____ to find out the population of the United States.

   Ⓐ almanacs   Ⓑ inquiries
   Ⓒ despots   Ⓓ improvisations

12. _____ the mystery of the missing lunch money was a difficult undertaking.

   Ⓐ Engineering   Ⓑ Positioning
   Ⓒ Universal   Ⓓ Unraveling

STOP!

Coast to Coast • Skills Assessment • Harcourt Brace School Publishers

COMPREHENSION: Make Predictions/Draw Conclusions

Directions: Read each passage. Fill in the answer circle in front of the correct answer for each question.

Sarah and Timothy planned to go horseback riding with their father on Sunday afternoon, but they had to finish their homework first. On Sunday morning Timothy began working on a book report that was due Monday. After finishing the first paragraph, he realized that the report was going to take him longer to write than he had thought. That afternoon Timothy was still working on his report when it was time to drive out to the stables. Sarah grabbed her coat and ran outside to meet her father, who was waiting in his truck.

13. What can you conclude about how Timothy spent Sunday afternoon?

Ⓐ He played in the back of his father's truck.
Ⓑ He worked with Sarah to finish his book report.
Ⓒ He finished writing his book report alone.
Ⓓ He went riding with Sarah and his father.

14. From this passage, you might predict that _____ .

Ⓐ Timothy will never write another book report again.
Ⓑ Sarah will go riding with her father on Monday.
Ⓒ The horses will be tired when Sarah and her father arrive at the stables.
Ⓓ Timothy will allow more time to write book reports in the future.

Coast to Coast • Skills Assessment • Harcourt Brace School Publishers

COMPREHENSION: Make Predictions/Draw Conclusions (continued)

Mrs. Halloway, the lunch monitor at Washington Elementary School, made sure the lunch room ran smoothly. She did not get too upset when things got a little noisy or something spilled, but she would not tolerate littering. If she saw a student drop something without picking it up, she'd walk up to that person and insist that he or she pick up the item and throw it in the trash can.

Mike and Toby were heading for their usual table. Mike was trying to carry his lunch tray in one hand and some books in the other. A napkin flew off his tray and landed on the floor. Mike didn't even notice it, but Mrs. Halloway did.

15. Mike and Toby probably _____ .

Ⓐ look alike
Ⓑ live on the same street
Ⓒ ride the school bus together
Ⓓ eat lunch together every day

16. From this passage you can predict that Mrs. Halloway will _____ .

Ⓐ change Mike's and Toby's seats
Ⓑ tell Mike to pick up the napkin
Ⓒ ask Toby to stay after school
Ⓓ punish Toby for making too much noise during lunch

Coast to Coast • Skills Assessment • Harcourt Brace School Publishers

STOP!

COMPREHENSION: Fact and Opinion/Author's Purpose and Viewpoint

Directions: Read each passage. Fill in the answer circle in front of the correct answer for each question.

Many people think that George Herman "Babe" Ruth was the greatest baseball player of all time. He set many records. For example, he hit 714 home runs during his career, and 60 in a single season. When he first started playing, he was a pitcher, and he set several pitching records. Later he became an outfielder and one of the most legendary hitters of all times. He was also an interesting and colorful character who was known for visiting sick children in hospitals and doing other kind deeds. However, he had a very difficult childhood and suffered from illnesses later in his life. Still, most people remember him as a great American hero. Although some of his records have since been broken, others still stand.

17. Which sentence states an <u>opinion</u> from the passage?
  Ⓐ He was a great American hero.
  Ⓑ He hit 60 home runs in a single season.
  Ⓒ When he started playing, he was a pitcher.
  Ⓓ His real name was George Herman Ruth.

18. The author wrote this paragraph to _____ .
  Ⓐ entertain
  Ⓑ inform
  Ⓒ persuade
  Ⓓ give directions

COMPREHENSION: Fact and Opinion/Author's Purpose and Viewpoint (continued)

On July 29, 1993 my cat Fluffy had a litter of five kittens. They were all beautiful, but one was much smaller than the others. It was also weaker than the other four and usually didn't get much milk from its mother because the other kittens kept pushing it away. My mother suggested feeding it with a baby bottle. We took great care of this little kitten that had become our favorite. After several weeks the little kitten had grown stronger. We named her Joy because we enjoyed her so much, and now, several years later, we still think Joy is the best cat in the world.

19. Which sentence states a <u>fact</u> from the passage?

Ⓐ All of Fluffy's kittens were beautiful.
Ⓑ Joy is the best cat in the world.
Ⓒ The other kittens were jealous of Joy.
Ⓓ The kittens were born on July 29.

20. The author's purpose in this passage was to ———.

Ⓐ inform
Ⓑ persuade
Ⓒ entertain
Ⓓ give directions

Coast to Coast • Skills Assessment • Harcourt Brace School Publishers

GO ON

COMPREHENSION: Fact and Opinion/Author's Purpose and Viewpoint (continued)

Carrie wanted to buy a special sweater for her mother's birthday, but she didn't have enough money. As Carrie walked home from school, she saw a wallet on the ground. She picked it up and looked inside. There were fifty dollars in the wallet! That was more than enough to buy her mother the beautiful sweater she had seen in the store window. Then Carrie looked through the rest of the wallet and found a driver's license. It belonged to Fred Blackwell and showed his address — 4286 South Oak Street. South Oak Street was right across the street. Carrie suddenly realized she couldn't keep the wallet. She crossed the street and rang the doorbell. A man answered the door, and Carrie asked, "Are you Mr. Blackwell?" The man said he was, and Carrie handed him his wallet. Mr. Blackwell was so happy to have his wallet back that he gave Carrie twenty dollars. Now Carrie could afford the beautiful sweater for her mother.

21. Which sentence states an <u>opinion</u> from the passage?

  Ⓐ Carrie saw a beautiful sweater in a store window.
  Ⓑ Carrie saw a wallet on the ground.
  Ⓒ Mr. Blackwell lives at 4286 South Oak Street.
  Ⓓ The wallet belonged to Fred Blackwell.

22. The author of this story probably believes that, _____ .

  Ⓐ "Easy does it."
  Ⓑ "Honesty is the best policy."
  Ⓒ "Finders keepers; losers weepers."
  Ⓓ "Every man for himself."

Coast to Coast • Skills Assessment • Harcourt Brace School Publishers

COMPREHENSION: Fact and Opinion/Author's Purpose and Viewpoint (continued)

> Monica was one of six finalists in the sixth-grade spelling bee. She expected the spelling words in the final round to be very difficult. On the way to the final competition, Monica's father told her that he and her mother were very proud of her and that, win or lose in today's contest, she would always be the best in their eyes. Monica believed she had the greatest parents in the world. She knew all they expected of her was that she do her best.

23. Which sentence states a <u>fact</u> from the passage?

    Ⓐ   Monica was an excellent speller.
    Ⓑ   There were six finalists in the spelling bee.
    Ⓒ   Monica had the greatest parents in the world.
    Ⓓ   The spelling words in the final round were very difficult.

24. The author of this passage wants the reader to know _____ .

    Ⓐ   how to study spelling words
    Ⓑ   how hard it is to win a spelling bee
    Ⓒ   how important it is to be good at spelling
    Ⓓ   how Monica and her parents feel about each other

Coast to Coast • Skills Assessment • Harcourt Brace School Publishers

STOP!

LANGUAGE ARTS

SKILLS

Recognize Complete and Simple
    Subjects and Predicates
Recognize Compound Subjects and
    Predicates
Recognize Simple and Compound
    Sentences and Conjunctions
Recognize Common and Proper
    Nouns

Criterion Score   12/16

Pupil Score   _____

Sample Multiple-Choice Questions:

The first kind of question is multiple choice. Carefully read the directions and the question. Then fill in the answer circle beside the choice you think is best. Question 1 has been answered for you. Look at it and then answer question 2.

Directions: Choose the **complete subject** of each sentence.

1. Tom ran to school.
    - Ⓐ Tom
    - Ⓑ ran

2. The cat slept on the chair.
    - Ⓐ The cat
    - Ⓑ slept on the chair

Sample Write-in-the-Answer Questions:

For the second kind of question, carefully read the directions and the question. Then write your answer on the line. Question 3 has been answered for you. Look at it and then answer question 4.

Directions: Write the **complete predicate** of each sentence.

3. We went to the ball game.

    went to the ball game
    _____

4. The game was exciting.

    _____

Coast to Coast • Skills Assessment • Harcourt Brace School Publishers

Directions: Choose the **simple subject** of this sentence. Fill in the answer circle beside the one you choose.

1. The stone walls around the garden were old and crumbling.

   Ⓐ stone
   Ⓑ walls
   Ⓒ garden

Directions: Choose the **simple predicate** of this sentence. Fill in the answer circle beside the one you choose.

2. Ferns grew in the shade.

   Ⓐ grew
   Ⓑ grew shade
   Ⓒ grew in the shade

Directions: Write the **complete predicate** of this sentence.

3. The cherry tree blossoms were falling like snow.

   _____

Directions: Write the **complete subject** of this sentence.

4. Red and white tulips bobbed in the warm spring breeze.

   _____

Directions: Decide whether each sentence has a **compound subject** or a **compound predicate.** Fill in the answer circle beside the one you choose.

5. The ducks and geese walked in single file down to the river.

   Ⓐ compound subject
   Ⓑ compound predicate

6. Rubber cement does a neater job and is much quicker.

   Ⓐ compound subject
   Ⓑ compound predicate

Coast to Coast • Skills Assessment • Harcourt Brace School Publishers

Directions: Write the **compound subject** of each sentence.

7. Swimming and sailing are my favorite water sports.

_____

8. The children and their friends called and called.

_____

Directions: Decide whether each sentence is a **simple sentence** or a **compound sentence.** Fill in the answer circle beside the one you choose.

9. Somebody left this book, but I don't know who it was.

Ⓐ simple sentence
Ⓑ compound sentence

10. Perhaps the owner of the book doesn't want it back.

Ⓐ simple sentence
Ⓑ compound sentence

Directions: Write the two **simple sentences** that form this compound sentence.

11. Ask Julie the question, but she might not know the answer.

_____

_____

Directions: Write the **conjunction** that joins these two simple sentences.

12. Mark brought the sandwiches, or maybe he helped with the salad.

_____

Coast to Coast • Skills Assessment • Harcourt Brace School Publishers

GO ON

Directions: Choose the **proper noun** to complete this sentence. Fill in the answer circle beside the one you choose.

13. Someone did a report on _____ .

   (A) sand sharks

   (B) William Shakespeare

Directions: Decide whether all the nouns in this sentence are **proper nouns** or **common nouns.** Fill in the answer circle beside the one you choose.

14. The Wilsons visited Washington in March.

   (A) proper nouns

   (B) common nouns

Directions: Write the **common nouns** in this sentence.

15. His grandmother left for her home in Georgia last Tuesday.

_____

Directions: Write the **proper nouns** in this sentence.

16. Old Faithful is the name of a geyser at Yellowstone National Park.

_____

American Portraits • Theme 2
Score _____

STOP!

13

Signatures

COAST TO COAST

SKILLS ASSESSMENT

AMERICAN PORTRAITS/THEME 2

HARCOURT BRACE

ORLANDO ATLANTA AUSTIN BOSTON SAN FRANCISCO CHICAGO DALLAS NEW YORK
TORONTO LONDON

PART NO. 9997-17412-7

ISBN 0-15-308236-4 (PACKAGE OF 12)

5

Skills Assessment: Reading and Language Arts

Coast to Coast/Theme 3

Name _____ Date _____

Reading

SKILL AREA	Criterion Score	Pupil Score	Pupil Strength
VOCABULARY Key Words	9/12		
LITERARY APPRECIATION Narrative Elements Plot, setting, character, theme	6/8		
STUDY SKILLS Reference Sources Dictionary, encyclopedia	3/4		
TOTAL SCORE	18/24		

HARCOURT BRACE

Copyright © by Harcourt Brace & Company

All rights reserved. No part of this publication may be reproduced
or transmitted in any form or by any means, electronic or mechanical, including
photocopy, recording, or any information storage and retrieval system.

Teachers using SIGNATURES may photocopy complete pages
in sufficient quantities for classroom use only and not for resale.

HARCOURT BRACE and Quill Design is a registered
trademark of Harcourt Brace & Company.

Printed in the United States of America

ISBN 0-15-308236-4

1 2 3 4 5 6 7 8 9 10 085 99 98 97 96

VOCABULARY: Key Words

Directions: Read each sentence. Fill in the answer circle in front of the word that best completes each sentence.

1. The thief was caught _____ goods across the border.

   (A) prospecting   (B) distinguishing
   (C) frequenting   (D) smuggling

2. My father warned us to stay away from the old, _____ house.

   (A) oppressed   (B) condemned
   (C) constant   (D) satisfied

3. I marked off my _____ by drawing a circle in the sand.

   (A) territory   (B) settler
   (C) recovery   (D) shade

4. My parents are going to listen to the presidential _____.

   (A) occupation   (B) convince
   (C) superior   (D) address

5. My aunt is trying to _____ a summer camp for children.

   (A) establish   (B) invest
   (C) evidence   (D) escape

6. Mark and his sister explored the college _____ together.

   (A) supply   (B) conceal
   (C) campus   (D) patrol

Coast to Coast • Skills Assessment • Harcourt Brace School Publishers

VOCABULARY: Key Words (continued)

7. The woman's _____ to the school was very generous.

   Ⓐ impression   Ⓑ donation
   Ⓒ debut   Ⓓ talent

8. Tracy _____ the house for her book, but she couldn't find it anywhere.

   Ⓐ rated   Ⓑ furiously
   Ⓒ paid   Ⓓ scoured

9. Paul mixed a _____ of mud, sand, and leaves in a bucket.

   Ⓐ rustle   Ⓑ scenery
   Ⓒ theory   Ⓓ concoction

10. Annie successfully _____ her bicycle through the tricky course.

   Ⓐ maneuvered   Ⓑ flew
   Ⓒ cautiously   Ⓓ survived

11. Although the instructions were _____ , Billy was able to build the model airplane.

   Ⓐ noticeable   Ⓑ dreaded
   Ⓒ supervised   Ⓓ vague

12. After the flood _____ , people returned to their homes.

   Ⓐ despaired   Ⓑ disrupted
   Ⓒ abated   Ⓓ improvised

STOP!

Coast to Coast • Skills Assessment • Harcourt Brace School Publishers

LITERARY APPRECIATION: Narrative Elements

Directions: Read each passage. Fill in the answer circle in front of the correct answer for each question.

Richard and his father sat on a dock by the lake near their campsite. They were hoping to catch fish for supper. However, neither of them had ever fished before, and they were not sure how to do it. Richard's father took a worm and tried wrapping it around his hook. Every time he thought the worm was on the hook, the worm fell off. Richard tried too, with the same unhappy results.

After a while they decided they needed some help. They walked along the edge of the lake in search of other campers, but the area was so vast and secluded that they never found anyone. Fishing would have to wait for another camping trip. Richard and his father returned to their tent site and unpacked sandwiches and chips from a bag. Richard was glad his mother had insisted on sending food.

13. The main characters in this story are a boy and his _____ .

   (A) mother   (B) father
   (C) brother   (D) friend

14. The beginning of this story takes place _____ .

   (A) on a dock   (B) on a boat
   (C) on an island   (D) in a field

15. The plot of this story is mostly about _____ .

   (A) how to find worms
   (B) the hazards of camping
   (C) family relationships
   (D) unsuccessful fishermen

16. Which is the best statement of the theme of this story?

   (A) "Be prepared."
   (B) "Never tell a lie."
   (C) "Things could always be worse."
   (D) "You can't teach an old dog new tricks."

Coast to Coast • Skills Assessment • Harcourt Brace School Publishers

GO ON

3

LITERARY APPRECIATION: Narrative Elements (continued)

> Kisha was babysitting little Ivan, the first infant she'd ever watched alone. Ivan's parents had gone to dinner and a show and would be home late. Everything started out fine. Kisha fed Ivan. Then she held the baby in her arms, rocked him, and sang to him. After Ivan fell asleep, she put him in his crib. Suddenly, however, Ivan woke up crying. Kisha picked him up and tried to calm him down. She sang more songs to him and bounced him in her arms, but nothing worked.
>
> Finally Kisha called her mother. She told her mother everything she had tried. Her mother listened patiently and then asked, "Have you changed his diaper tonight?" Kisha felt foolish. That was the problem. In five minutes Ivan was happy and dry.

17. The main characters in this story are Ivan and his _____ .

   (A) father
   (B) mother
   (C) sister
   (D) babysitter

18. This story takes place _____ .

   (A) at Ivan's house
   (B) in a restaurant
   (C) at a show
   (D) at a day care center

19. The plot of this story is mostly about how Kisha _____ .

   (A) discovered Ivan's problem
   (B) earned extra money
   (C) helped her mother
   (D) sang songs

20. Which is the best statement of the theme of this story?

   (A) Rock-a-by baby.
   (B) Mother knows best.
   (C) You can't be too careful.
   (D) Children should be seen and not heard.

Coast to Coast • Skills Assessment • Harcourt Brace School Publishers

STUDY SKILLS: Reference Sources

Directions: Look at the set of encyclopedia. Then read the article. Fill in the answer circle in front of the correct answer for each question.

ENCYCLOPEDIA

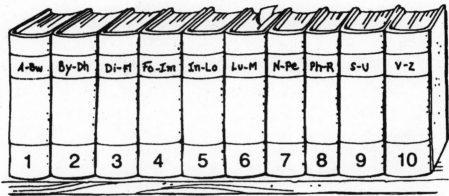

ROCK MUSIC Rock music has been the dominant pop-music style since the late 1950s. The first national rock music hit was "Rock Around the Clock," by Bill Haley and the Comets in 1955. Rock's first superstar was Elvis Presley, who concocted his own rock music style by combining rock music with rhythm-and-blues and country and western music. Bill Haley and the Comets, Elvis Presley, and many other rock music stars are remembered in the Rock and Roll Hall of Fame, which opened in Cleveland, Ohio, in 1995.

See also Presley; Beatles; Country and Western Music

21. The main article about rock music could be found in volume _____ .

   (A) 3
   (C) 8
   (B) 5
   (D) 10

22. Additional information on this subject could be found in volume _____ .

   (A) 2
   (C) 5
   (B) 4
   (D) 9

Coast to Coast • Skills Assessment • Harcourt Brace School Publishers

STUDY SKILLS: Reference Sources (continued)

Directions: Look at this part of a page from a dictionary. Then read the questions. Fill in the answer circle in front of the correct answer for each question.

history   **hitch**

his·to·ry [his´tə·rē] *n., pl.* **his·to·ries**
1 Past events or a record of them, often concerning a particular nation, people, or activity: European *history;* the *history* of art.   **2** The branch of knowledge that deals with past events.   **3** An interesting past: That house has quiate a *history.*

his·tri·on·ic [his´trē·on´ik] *adj.*   **1** Having to do with actors or acting.   **2** Affected; insincere.

his·tri·on·ics [his´trē·on´iks] *n.pl.* Exaggerated display of emotion to gain the attention or sympathy of others.

hit [hit] *v.* **hit, hit·ting,** *n.*   **1** To give a blow to or make forceful contact with; strike: to *hit* a ball; The car *hit* the tree.   **2** *v.* To reach or strike, as

with a shot from a gun: to *hit* the tar-get.   **3** *n.* Something, as a blow or shot, that reaches its target.   **4** *v.* To have a bad effect on; cause to suffer: Misfortune *hit* the company hard.   **5** *v.* To come upon or discover: to *hit* the main road; to *hit* upon an idea.   **6** *n.* A great success: The song was a *hit.*   **7** *n.* In baseball, a base hit.   **8** *v.* To bat. —**hit if off** To get on well together. —**hit´ter** *n.*

hitch [hich]   **1** *v.* To fasten or tie: to *hitch* a rope to a post; to *hitch* up a horse.   **2** *n.* A thing used to hitch, as one of various knots.   **3** *n.* A coupling; fastening.   **4** *v.* T become fastened or snarled: Moorings fouled and *hitched.*

23.   The guide words on this page are _____ .

(A) himself - hitting   (B) history - hitch
(C) hit - hitch   (D) himself - hit

24.   Which meaning of <u>hit</u> is used in the phrase, "a hit movie"?

(A) 1   (B) 2
(C) 3   (D) 6

STOP!

Coast to Coast • Skills Assessment • Harcourt Brace School Publishers

LANGUAGE ARTS

SKILLS

Recognize Singular and Plural Nouns
Recognize Possessive Nouns
Recognize Pronouns and Antecedents
Recognize Subject, Object, Reflexive,
    and Possessive Pronouns

Criterion Score	12/16
Pupil Score	_____

Coast to Coast • Skills Assessment • Harcourt Brace School Publishers

Sample Multiple-Choice Questions:

The first kind of question is multiple choice. Carefully read the directions and the question. Then fill in the answer circle beside the choice you think is best. Question 1 has been answered for you. Look at it and then answer question 2.

Directions: Choose the **complete subject** of each sentence.

1. Tom ran to school.
    - Ⓐ Tom
    - Ⓑ ran

2. The cat slept on the chair.
    - Ⓐ The cat
    - Ⓑ slept on the chair

Sample Write-in-the-Answer Questions:

For the second kind of question, carefully read the directions and the question. Then write your answer on the line. Question 3 has been answered for you. Look at it and then answer question 4.

Directions: Write the **complete predicate** of each sentence.

3. We went to the ball game.

    went to the ball game
    _____

4. The game was exciting.

    _____

Coast to Coast • Skills Assessment • Harcourt Brace School Publishers

Directions: Decide whether all the **nouns** in this sentence are **singular** or **plural**. Fill in the answer circle beside the one you choose.

1. Charla banged on the drum while her sister and brother sang.

   Ⓐ singular
   Ⓑ plural

Directions: Choose the **plural noun** in this sentence. Fill in the answer circle beside the one you choose.

2. The ducks walked down the hill and paddled across the lake.

   Ⓐ ducks
   Ⓑ hill
   Ⓒ lake

Directions: Write the **singular nouns** in this sentence.

3. His son could see three frogs on the bottom.

   _____

Directions: Rewrite this sentence to make the **nouns plural**.

4. The robin perched on the branch.

   _____

Coast to Coast • Skills Assessment • Harcourt Brace School Publishers

Directions: Choose the **possessive noun** in this sentence. Fill in the answer circle beside the one you choose.

5. I was surprised that she drove Mel's car.

   Ⓐ I
   Ⓑ she
   Ⓒ Mel's

Directions: Rewrite the **possessive nouns** in this sentence correctly.

6. The imprint on the childrens shirts said "Chicagos Best."

   _____

Directions: Choose the correct way to rewrite the underlined phrase in each sentence by using a **possessive noun.**

7. The manes of the horses were white with snow.

   Ⓐ horse's manes
   Ⓑ horses' manes
   Ⓒ horses mane's

8. There's gold at the end of the rainbow.

   Ⓐ the rainbows' end
   Ⓑ the rain bow's
   Ⓒ the rainbow's end

Coast to Coast • Skills Assessment • Harcourt Brace School Publishers

GO ON

Directions: Choose the **pronoun** that best replaces the underlined words in each sentence. Fill in the answer circle beside the one you choose.

9. <u>Petra and J.R.</u> wanted to borrow our bikes.

   Ⓐ Them
   Ⓑ Us
   Ⓒ They

10. That telephone call was for <u>Rosa</u>.

   Ⓐ her
   Ⓑ we
   Ⓒ his

Directions: Choose the **antecedent** of the **pronoun** in this sentence. Fill in the answer circle beside the one you choose.

11. Marshall wanted to go along, but he got home after Joy left.

   Ⓐ Marshall
   Ⓑ but
   Ⓒ Joy

Directions: Write the four **pronouns** in this sentence.

12. We weren't sure if he himself knew where to find them.

_____

Coast to Coast • Skills Assessment • Harcourt Brace School Publishers

Directions: Decide whether the underlined word is a **subject pronoun**, an **object pronoun**, a **reflexive pronoun**, or a **possessive pronoun**. Fill in the answer circle beside the one you choose.

13. We saw the plane go down <u>ourselves</u>.

    Ⓐ subject pronoun
    Ⓑ object pronoun
    Ⓒ reflexive pronoun
    Ⓓ possessive pronoun

14. <u>He</u> spent weeks in the wilderness.

    Ⓐ subject pronoun
    Ⓑ object pronoun
    Ⓒ reflexive pronoun
    Ⓓ possessive pronoun

Directions: Write the **object pronoun** in this sentence.

15. He realized that almost nothing scared him.

_____

Directions: Write the **subject pronoun** in this sentence.

16. We won't come until Nina herself calls us.

_____

Coast to Coast • Skills Assessment • Harcourt Brace School Publishers

STOP!

Signatures

COAST TO COAST

SKILLS ASSESSMENT

PERSONAL JOURNEYS/THEME 3

HARCOURT
BRACE

ORLANDO ATLANTA AUSTIN BOSTON SAN FRANCISCO CHICAGO DALLAS NEW YORK
TORONTO LONDON

PART NO. 9997-17413-5

ISBN 0-15-308236-4   (PACKAGE OF 12)
5

Signatures

Skills Assessment: Reading and Language Arts

Coast to Coast/Theme 4

Name _____ Date _____

Reading

Skill Area	Criterion Score	Pupil Score	Pupil Strength
VOCABULARY			
Key Words	9/12		
Context Clues/Multiple-meaning Words	6/8		
COMPREHENSION			
Compare and Contrast	3/4		
TOTAL SCORE	18/24		

HARCOURT BRACE

Copyright © by Harcourt Brace & Company

All rights reserved. No part of this publication may be reproduced or transmitted in any form or by any means, electronic or mechanical, including photocopy, recording, or any information storage and retrieval system.

Teachers using SIGNATURES may photocopy complete pages in sufficient quantities for classroom use only and not for resale.

HARCOURT BRACE and Quill Design is a registered trademark of Harcourt Brace & Company.

Printed in the United States of America

ISBN 0-15-308236-4

1 2 3 4 5 6 7 8 9 10   085   99 98 97 96

VOCABULARY: Key Words

Directions: Read each sentence. Fill in the answer circle in front of the word that best completes each sentence.

1. The reporter focused her article _____ on the town's problems.

   Ⓐ determination   Ⓑ horizontally
   Ⓒ firm   Ⓓ exclusively

2. The dog did not bark because it was _____ .

   Ⓐ timidly   Ⓑ mute
   Ⓒ oppression   Ⓓ noticeable

3. Lizzie was _____ the question by pretending not to have heard it.

   Ⓐ evading   Ⓑ indicating
   Ⓒ supervising   Ⓓ treatment

4. I don't like it when people try to _____ their beliefs on me.

   Ⓐ appeal   Ⓑ haze
   Ⓒ superior   Ⓓ impose

5. Dana _____ a class rule by calling out without raising her hand.

   Ⓐ engaged   Ⓑ instigated
   Ⓒ violated   Ⓓ stimulated

6. My dad used his _____ to convince people to vote for building a new school.

   Ⓐ influence   Ⓑ rustle
   Ⓒ conquer   Ⓓ inspection

Coast to Coast • Skills Assessment • Harcourt Brace School Publishers

GO ON   1

VOCABULARY: Key Words (continued)

7. Nancy was so proud after her successful piano _____ .

   (A) perform   (B) culture
   (C) recital   (D) veranda

8. My grandma _____ the bread dough with her hands.

   (A) enchanted   (B) kneaded
   (C) complimented   (D) resembled

9. Before I play a song on the piano, I always practice the _____ .

   (A) scales   (B) prodigies
   (C) improvise   (D) characters

10. The robot had a _____ voice.

    (A) exhibition   (B) dignity
    (C) peculiar   (D) endangered

11. When he blows into that trumpet, he makes a _____ noise.

    (A) spiral   (B) flax
    (C) dreadful   (D) conscious

12. Your kind words were greatly _____ .

    (A) talented   (B) appreciated
    (C) indifferent   (D) shriveled

STOP!

Coast to Coast • Skills Assessment • Harcourt Brace School Publishers

VOCABULARY: Context Clues/Multiple-meaning Words

Directions: Read each passage. Fill in the answer circle in front of the correct answer for each question.

Did you know you eat sodium every day? Sodium is a mineral that occurs naturally in some foods and is often added to foods and beverages for taste. For example, sodium is added to most canned vegetables, sauces, soups, and salad dressings. Most of the sodium in our diets comes from table salt, which contains quite a bit of sodium. Our bodies need sodium, but not very much. In fact, most Americans consume too much sodium. Most of us need only a minute amount of sodium each day. It is needed to help us maintain normal blood volume and blood pressure.

13. The word table in this passage means _____ .

    (A) having to do with food
    (B) to put something aside until later
    (C) a chart for showing data
    (D) the level of underground water

14. The word consume in this passage means _____ .

    (A) to take up one's attention
    (B) to eat or drink
    (C) to spend
    (D) to destroy

15. The word minute in this passage means _____ .

    (A) part of an hour
    (B) a dance
    (C) very small
    (D) not important

16. The word maintain in this passage means _____ .

    (A) to keep in good condition
    (B) to insist something is true
    (C) to pay expenses for something
    (D) to repair something

Coast to Coast • Skills Assessment • Harcourt Brace School Publishers

VOCABULARY: Context Clues/Multiple-meaning Words (continued)

France is not the only country in which French is spoken. Canada, just north of the United States, has many French-speaking citizens as well. In fact, French is one of Canada's two <u>official</u> languages. The other official language of Canada is English. The Canadian province Quebec has the largest French-speaking population of North America. A majority of the citizens of Quebec are <u>native</u> speakers of French. Quebec has even <u>passed</u> laws to give French a privileged status, in an effort to <u>preserve</u> Quebec's distinct culture and heritage.

17. The word <u>official</u> in this passage means _____ .

   Ⓐ a police officer
   Ⓑ an umpire or referee
   Ⓒ recognized or authorized
   Ⓓ not fake

18. The word <u>native</u> in this passage means _____ .

   Ⓐ belonging to a person's place of birth
   Ⓑ plants grown in an area
   Ⓒ natural or normal
   Ⓓ dating from the distant past

19. The word <u>passed</u> in this passage means _____ .

   Ⓐ to make into law
   Ⓑ to ignore
   Ⓒ to go beyond
   Ⓓ a ticket of admission

20. The word <u>preserve</u> in this passage means _____ .

   Ⓐ fruit cooked to make jelly
   Ⓑ to keep food from spoiling
   Ⓒ an area for wildlife
   Ⓓ to protect or continue

STOP!

Coast to Coast • Skills Assessment • Harcourt Brace School Publishers

COMPREHENSION: Compare and Contrast

Directions: Read the passage. Fill in the answer circle in front of the correct answer for each question.

Mars, the fourth planet from the sun, is on the other side of the earth from Venus. It has a cratered surface marked with canyons and ancient volcanoes. Mars has two moons named Phobos and Deimos. Venus, the third planet from the sun, has no moons. Venus is slightly smaller than Earth and covered by dense clouds. The planet with the most moons is Saturn. It has more than 20 moons. Saturn is the second largest planet and is the sixth planet from the sun. Jupiter is the largest planet. It is larger than all the other planets combined. Jupiter has sixteen known moons, two of which are larger than the planet Mercury, the planet closest to the sun.

21. According to the passage, Saturn and Mars are alike in that they both have _____ .

   Ⓐ moons
   Ⓑ dense clouds
   Ⓒ craters
   Ⓓ rings

22. Compared to Venus, Saturn _____ .

   Ⓐ has fewer moons
   Ⓑ is smaller
   Ⓒ is further from the sun
   Ⓓ is cloudier

23. Jupiter is different from all of the other planets, because it _____ .

   Ⓐ is the largest
   Ⓑ has the most moons
   Ⓒ has ancient volcanoes
   Ⓓ is closest to the sun

24. One way in which Jupiter and Saturn are alike is that they both _____ .

   Ⓐ have the same number of moons
   Ⓑ are smaller than Venus
   Ⓒ are larger than Earth
   Ⓓ are closer to the sun than Mercury

Coast to Coast • Skills Assessment • Harcourt Brace School Publishers

STOP!   5

LANGUAGE ARTS

SKILLS

Recognize Adjectives and Articles
Recognize Proper Adjectives
Recognize Comparing Adjectives
Recognize Action and Linking Verbs
Recognize Main Verbs and Helping
   Verbs

Criterion Score	15/20
Pupil Score	_____

Coast to Coast • Skills Assessment • Harcourt Brace School Publishers

Sample Multiple-Choice Questions:

The first kind of question is multiple choice. Carefully read the directions and the question. Then fill in the answer circle beside the choice you think is best. Question 1 has been answered for you. Look at it and then answer question 2.

Directions: Choose the **complete subject** of each sentence.

1. Tom ran to school.

    (A) Tom
    (B) ran

2. The cat slept on the chair.

    (A) The cat
    (B) slept on the chair

Sample Write-in-the-Answer Questions:

For the second kind of question, carefully read the directions and the question. Then write your answer on the line. Question 3 has been answered for you. Look at it and then answer question 4.

Directions: Write the **complete predicate** of each sentence.

3. We went to the ball game.

    went to the ball game

4. The game was exciting.

    _____

Coast to Coast • Skills Assessment • Harcourt Brace School Publishers

Directions: Choose the **article** in this sentence. Fill in the answer circle beside the one you choose.

1. I brought a new green wool sweater.

   Ⓐ a
   Ⓑ new
   Ⓒ green

Directions: Choose the **adjective** in this sentence. Fill in the answer circle beside the one you choose.

2. Parrots can be noisy pets that disturb the neighbors.

   Ⓐ Parrots
   Ⓑ noisy
   Ⓒ pets

Directions: Write the two **adjectives** in each sentence.

3. You can see that the black shoes won't fit her tiny feet.

   _____

4. The unpaved street is filled with many potholes.

   _____

Coast to Coast • Skills Assessment • Harcourt Brace School Publishers

Directions: Choose the word that is the **proper adjective** in each sentence. Fill in the answer circle beside the one you choose.

5. My Canadian pen pal lives in a house near Montreal.

   Ⓐ Canadian
   Ⓑ pen pal
   Ⓒ Montreal

6. Her family comes from Russia and her great-grandfather was born in Poland, but she has mostly French neighbors.

   Ⓐ Russia
   Ⓑ Poland
   Ⓒ French

Directions: Write the two **proper adjectives** in this sentence.

7. Japanese rice cakes taste good with Chinese tea.

   _____

Directions: Rewrite this sentence to correct the **capitalization**.

8. We ate italian sausage and spanish rice.

   _____

Coast to Coast • Skills Assessment • Harcourt Brace School Publishers

Directions: Choose the correct form of the **adjective** to go in each blank. Fill in the answer circle beside the one you choose.

9. It was the _____ day Goldilocks had ever had.

Ⓐ bad
Ⓑ worse
Ⓒ worst

10. This bowl of porridge is _____ than that one.

Ⓐ warm
Ⓑ warmer
Ⓒ warmest

11. Papa Bear's chair was the _____ of the three chairs.

Ⓐ comfortable
Ⓑ more comfortable
Ⓒ most comfortable

12. Gino was young, but his brother Joseph was even _____ .

Ⓐ young
Ⓑ younger
Ⓒ youngest

GO ON

Coast to Coast • Skills Assessment • Harcourt Brace School Publishers

Directions: Choose the **linking verb** in each sentence. Fill in the answer circle beside the one you choose.

13. This is the last day of the week.

Ⓐ is
Ⓑ week
Ⓒ last

14. Insects are cold-blooded animals.

Ⓐ are
Ⓑ slow
Ⓒ falls

Directions: Choose the **action verb** in this compound sentence. Fill in the answer circle beside the one you choose.

15. After his tenth birthday, Zane's family moved.

Ⓐ after
Ⓑ moved

Directions: Write the **action verb** in this sentence.

16. The chirps of a snowy tree cricket indicate the temperature.

_____

Coast to Coast • Skills Assessment • Harcourt Brace School Publishers

Directions: Decide whether the underlined word in each sentence is a **helping verb** or a **main verb**. Fill in the answer circle beside the one you choose.

17. I <u>will</u> finish my homework after supper.

   Ⓐ helping verb
   Ⓑ main verb

18. Should Charlie <u>bring</u> your notebook?

   Ⓐ helping verb
   Ⓑ main verb

Directions: Write the **helping verb** in this sentence.

19. That elephant does walk a little faster than the others.

   _____

Directions: Write the **main verb** in this sentence.

20. My children have always brought me flowers.

   _____

Coast to Coast • Skills Assessment • Harcourt Brace School Publishers

Signatures

Coast to Coast

Skills Assessment

Listen to This!/Theme 4

HARCOURT BRACE

ORLANDO ATLANTA AUSTIN BOSTON SAN FRANCISCO CHICAGO DALLAS NEW YORK
TORONTO LONDON

PART NO. 9997-17414-3

ISBN 0-15-308236-4   (PACKAGE OF 12)

5

Signatures

Skills Assessment: Reading and Language Arts

Coast to Coast/Theme 5

Name _____ Date _____

Reading

SKILL AREA	Criterion Score	Pupil Score	Pupil Strength
DECODING Structural Analysis Prefixes, suffixes, roots	6/8		
VOCABULARY Key Words	9/12		
COMPREHENSION Main Idea and Details	3/4		
TOTAL SCORE	18/24		

HARCOURT BRACE

Copyright © by Harcourt Brace & Company

All rights reserved. No part of this publication may be reproduced
or transmitted in any form or by any means, electronic or mechanical, including
photocopy, recording, or any information storage and retrieval system.

Teachers using SIGNATURES may photocopy complete pages
in sufficient quantities for classroom use only and not for resale.

HARCOURT BRACE and Quill Design is a registered
trademark of Harcourt Brace & Company.

Printed in the United States of America

ISBN 0-15-308236-4

1 2 3 4 5 6 7 8 9 10 085 99 98 97 96

DECODING: Structural Analysis

Directions: Read each sentence. Fill in the answer circle in front of the word that best completes each sentence.

1. I was not at all _____ with your sloppy work.

   Ⓐ satisfactory
   Ⓑ satisfied
   Ⓒ dissatisfaction
   Ⓓ dissatisfied

2. Molly becomes very _____ when someone criticizes her.

   Ⓐ defend
   Ⓑ defended
   Ⓒ defensive
   Ⓓ defensible

3. Roger noticed that flowers _____ bees.

   Ⓐ attract
   Ⓑ attraction
   Ⓒ attractive
   Ⓓ unattractive

4. The coach tries to _____ negative thinking.

   Ⓐ courage
   Ⓑ discourage
   Ⓒ encouragement
   Ⓓ discouragement

Coast to Coast • Skills Assessment • Harcourt Brace School Publishers

DECODING: Structural Analysis (continued)

5. My sister was lucky to find _____ with an excellent company.

   Ⓐ employ
   Ⓑ employer
   Ⓒ employee
   Ⓓ employment

6. When Tammy feels sluggish, she tries to _____ herself by eating a healthful snack.

   Ⓐ energetic
   Ⓑ energize
   Ⓒ energy
   Ⓓ energizer

7. We had _____ problems with that old car.

   Ⓐ discontinue
   Ⓑ continue
   Ⓒ continually
   Ⓓ continuous

8. I have a _____ that something is missing.

   Ⓐ suspect
   Ⓑ suspicion
   Ⓒ suspense
   Ⓓ suspicious

STOP!

Coast to Coast • Skills Assessment • Harcourt Brace School Publishers

VOCABULARY: Key Words

Directions: Read each sentence. Fill in the answer circle in front of the word that best completes each sentence.

9. Eric decided to _____ his vacation day to help paint his neighbor's house.

   Ⓐ kindness   Ⓑ sacrifice
   Ⓒ determine   Ⓓ occupy

10. The people _____ the day on which their town was founded.

   Ⓐ stunned   Ⓑ composed
   Ⓒ endangered   Ⓓ commemorated

11. After the _____ , the park was a clean, safe place again.

   Ⓐ commercial   Ⓑ orderly
   Ⓒ restoration   Ⓓ rhythm

12. The _____ of books to students takes place during the first week of school.

   Ⓐ distribution   Ⓑ tradition
   Ⓒ exhibition   Ⓓ culture

13. Many animals _____ these woods.

   Ⓐ breed   Ⓑ provide
   Ⓒ inhabit   Ⓓ observe

14. The new factory had a big _____ on the town.

   Ⓐ stimulate   Ⓑ dignity
   Ⓒ impact   Ⓓ satisfaction

Coast to Coast • Skills Assessment • Harcourt Brace School Publishers

GO ON

3

VOCABULARY: Key Words (continued)

---

15. The _____ old building was going to be torn down.

   (A) desolate   (B) indifferent
   (C) despair   (D) inspiration

---

16. The only kind of meat Jack will eat is _____ .

   (A) herbs   (B) prospecting
   (C) poultry   (D) nectar

---

17. I have trouble understanding the _____ spoken in that region.

   (A) detection   (B) dialect
   (C) observation   (D) cycle

---

18. We will not _____ littering in our community.

   (A) tolerate   (B) monitor
   (C) offensive   (D) officially

---

19. The Egyptian pyramids _____ the memory of the pharaohs.

   (A) decipher   (B) necessitate
   (C) excuse   (D) perpetuate

---

20. Jill always _____ the importance of being careful and taking precautions.

   (A) estimates   (B) annoys
   (C) pressures   (D) emphasizes

STOP!

Coast to Coast • Skills Assessment • Harcourt Brace School Publishers

COMPREHENSION: Main Idea and Details

> **Directions:** Read the passage. Fill in the answer circle in front of the correct answer for each question.

Winter, spring, summer, fall. The four seasons come and go, but have you ever wondered *why* we have seasons? Contrary to what some people believe, our seasons are not caused by the fact that the Earth's orbit around the Sun is an ellipse—an oval shape. Instead, the seasons are caused by the tilt of the Earth's axis. The Earth's axis is an imaginary line that goes through the center of the Earth, beginning at the North Pole and ending at the South Pole. When the northern end of the Earth's axis tilts away from the Sun, the southern axis is tilting toward the Sun. That makes it colder in the northern hemisphere, so you have winter. At the same time, it is warmer in the southern hemisphere, so people there have summer.

21. What is the main idea of this passage?

   Ⓐ Summer is a season.
   Ⓑ We do not understand what causes our seasons.
   Ⓒ Seasons are caused by the tilt of Earth's axis.
   Ⓓ People live in the northern hemisphere.

22. Which of the following details best supports the main idea?

   Ⓐ The Earth's axis is an imaginary line.
   Ⓑ The seasons come and go.
   Ⓒ The Earth's orbit is an ellipse.
   Ⓓ The northern axis tilts away from the Sun during winter.

23. It is winter in the southern hemisphere when _____ .

   Ⓐ the southern axis tilts away from the Sun
   Ⓑ the southern axis tilts toward the Sun
   Ⓒ the northern axis tilts away from the Sun
   Ⓓ Earth's axis is not tilted

24. When it is winter in the northern hemisphere, what season is it in the southern hemisphere?

   Ⓐ winter
   Ⓑ spring
   Ⓒ summer
   Ⓓ fall

Coast to Coast • Skills Assessment • Harcourt Brace School Publishers

LANGUAGE ARTS

SKILLS

Recognize Correct Verb Tenses
Recognize Present Tense and Past
  Tense Verbs
Recognize Irregular Verbs
Recognize Future Tense Verbs

Criterion Score   12/16

Pupil Score   _____

Coast to Coast • Skills Assessment • Harcourt Brace School Publishers

Sample Multiple-Choice Questions:

The first kind of question is multiple choice. Carefully read the directions and the question. Then fill in the answer circle beside the choice you think is best. Question 1 has been answered for you. Look at it and then answer question 2.

Directions: Choose the **complete subject** of each sentence.

1.   Tom ran to school.

     Ⓐ Tom
     Ⓑ ran

2.   The cat slept on the chair.

     Ⓐ The cat
     Ⓑ slept on the chair

Sample Write-in-the-Answer Questions:

For the second kind of question, carefully read the directions and the question. Then write your answer on the line. Question 3 has been answered for you. Look at it and then answer question 4.

Directions: Write the **complete predicate** of each sentence.

3.   We went to the ball game.

    went to the ball game

4.   The game was exciting.

    _____

Coast to Coast • Skills Assessment • Harcourt Brace School Publishers

Directions: Decide whether each sentence is in the **past, present,** or **future tense.** Fill in the answer circle beside the one you choose.

1. You will find many interesting seaweeds on the beach.

   (A) past tense
   (B) present tense
   (C) future tense

2. Look for the sea oak, which resembles a red oak leaf.

   (A) past tense
   (B) present tense
   (C) future tense

3. Sea oaks grow on other seaweeds, such as kelp.

   (A) past tense
   (B) present tense
   (C) future tense

Directions: Write the two **verbs** in this sentence that are in the **past tense.**

4. My friend Shantelle cooked some kelp, and I tasted it.

   _____

Coast to Coast • Skills Assessment • Harcourt Brace School Publishers

GO ON

Directions: Choose the correct form of the **verb** to complete each sentence. Fill in the answer circle beside the one you choose.

5. The lumber was _____ in a drying room, called a kiln.

    Ⓐ dries
    Ⓑ dried
    Ⓒ dry

6. Mark has _____ many mistakes in this article.

    Ⓐ find
    Ⓑ found
    Ⓒ finding

Directions: Choose the **present tense** of the **verb** to complete the sentence.

7. Jonelle _____ up her paintings.

    Ⓐ box
    Ⓑ boxes
    Ⓒ boxing

Directions: Write the **past tense** of the underlined **verb**.

8. Gail went right outside and <u>call</u> them.

_____

GO ON

Coast to Coast • Skills Assessment • Harcourt Brace School Publishers

Directions: Write the **present tense** of the underlined **verb**.

9. Everyone <u>wish</u> on a star at least once in a lifetime.

_____

Directions: Choose the **irregular verb** in this compound sentence. Fill in the answer circle beside the one you choose.

10. Geo and Liz carry the food, we bring the lawn chairs, and Hosea and his brother help with the drinks.

Ⓐ carry
Ⓑ bring
Ⓒ help

Directions: Write the **past-tense** of the **verb** in this sentence.

11. We never stand still!

_____

Directions: Rewrite this sentence to correct the underlined **verbs**.

12. <u>Sit</u> the alarm clock on the table before you <u>lay</u> down.

_____

Coast to Coast • Skills Assessment • Harcourt Brace School Publishers

Directions: Choose whether the underlined **verb** shows a **past, future,** or **present action.** Fill in the answer circle beside the one you choose.

13. Lily <u>will participate</u> in the Special Olympics this year.

    Ⓐ past action
    Ⓑ future action
    Ⓒ present action

Directions: Choose the **future tense** of the **verb** in this sentence. Fill in the answer circle beside the one you choose.

14. My family will never move to a cold climate.

    Ⓐ will move
    Ⓑ never move
    Ⓒ move to

Directions: Rewrite each sentence so the **verb** is in the **future tense.**

15. Mary is writing to her parents.

_____

16. Ken hits the puck into the net!

_____

Coast to Coast • Skills Assessment • Harcourt Brace School Publishers

Signatures

COAST TO COAST

SKILLS ASSESSMENT

PLANET OF LIFE/THEME 5

HARCOURT
BRACE

ORLANDO ATLANTA AUSTIN BOSTON SAN FRANCISCO CHICAGO DALLAS NEW YORK
TORONTO LONDON

PART NO. 9997-17415-1

ISBN 0-15-308236-4   (PACKAGE OF 12)

5

Signatures

Skills Assessment: Reading and Language Arts

Coast to Coast/Theme 6

Name _____ Date _____

Reading

SKILL AREA	Criterion Score	Pupil Score	Pupil Strength
VOCABULARY Key Words	12/16	_____	_____
COMPREHENSION Summarize/Paraphrase	6/8	_____	_____
TOTAL SCORE	18/24	_____	_____

HARCOURT BRACE

Copyright © by Harcourt Brace & Company

All rights reserved. No part of this publication may be reproduced
or transmitted in any form or by any means, electronic or mechanical, including
photocopy, recording, or any information storage and retrieval system.

Teachers using SIGNATURES may photocopy complete pages
in sufficient quantities for classroom use only and not for resale.

HARCOURT BRACE and Quill Design is a registered
trademark of Harcourt Brace & Company.

Printed in the United States of America

ISBN 0-15-308236-4

1 2 3 4 5 6 7 8 9 10 085 99 98 97 96

VOCABULARY: Key Words

Directions: Read each sentence. Fill in the answer circle in front of the word that best completes each sentence.

1. We elected him to be our _____ in Washington.

   Ⓐ patient   Ⓑ impression
   Ⓒ confident   Ⓓ spokesperson

2. The boy did not have _____ training in music.

   Ⓐ partial   Ⓑ culture
   Ⓒ formal   Ⓓ reliable

3. Wearing a uniform is _____ in some schools.

   Ⓐ compulsory   Ⓑ reluctant
   Ⓒ irritated   Ⓓ minimal

4. The job pays $200 a week plus free _____ .

   Ⓐ assault and battery   Ⓑ room and board
   Ⓒ determination   Ⓓ occupation

5. Paula came up with the _____ idea that saved the day.

   Ⓐ ingenious   Ⓑ heroine
   Ⓒ cautiously   Ⓓ many

6. We saw several _____ fields among the wood lots.

   Ⓐ chanting   Ⓑ legendary
   Ⓒ rustle   Ⓓ cultivated

Coast to Coast • Skills Assessment • Harcourt Brace School Publishers

GO ON

1

VOCABULARY: Key Words (continued)

7. My parents attempted to _____ my confidence before I performed on stage.

   (A) bolster   (B) emerge
   (C) counter   (D) grant

8. We are _____ to know how our tax dollars are spent.

   (A) conscious   (B) dreaded
   (C) entitled   (D) stunning

9. This organization was _____ in 1942.

   (A) founded   (B) improvised
   (C) indicated (D) lower

10. This painting is my greatest _____ .

    (A) eagerly   (B) audition
    (C) accomplishment   (D) succeed

11. The _____ soldiers traveled on foot, while horses carried the wounded.

    (A) victim   (B) able-bodied
    (C) well-respected (D) artificial

12. We discussed the _____ of the new rules.

    (A) superiors   (B) ebb and flow
    (C) pros and cons (D) satisfaction

Coast to Coast • Skills Assessment • Harcourt Brace School Publishers

VOCABULARY: Key Words (continued)

13. The _____ of the town voted for a new mayor.

    Ⓐ citizens   Ⓑ heritage
    Ⓒ hostility   Ⓓ locale

14. My _____ came to the United States from Europe.

    Ⓐ dexterity   Ⓑ ancestors
    Ⓒ colony   Ⓓ dignity

15. There were no stores in the _____ neighborhood.

    Ⓐ residential   Ⓑ commercial
    Ⓒ symmetrical   Ⓓ chronic

16. She runs a _____ company that has grown every year.

    Ⓐ translated   Ⓑ prosperous
    Ⓒ deserted   Ⓓ stagnant

Coast to Coast • Skills Assessment • Harcourt Brace School Publishers

COMPREHENSION: Summarize/Paraphrase

Directions: Read each passage. Fill in the answer circle in front of the correct answer for each question.

Denise was excited when her teacher announced that her class would put on a production of *The Wizard of Oz*. Denise announced that she'd like to be the cowardly lion.

"You can't be the cowardly lion!" Jerry protested. "The cowardly lion is a boy, and you're a girl."

"What difference does it make?" Denise replied. "If I can play the role well, then it shouldn't make any difference."

Denise's teacher agreed. "Denise can try out for the part. The play is a fantasy story anyway. If Denise can learn the lines and play the part, it doesn't matter whether the character is played by a girl or a boy. What's more important is that we all work hard and have fun."

Once that was settled, tryouts began and they proceeded to cast the play.

17. Which of the following statements best summarizes this passage?

Ⓐ Denise is someone who always gets her way.
Ⓑ Denise's class decided to put on a production of *The Wizard of Oz*.
Ⓒ In this fantasy play, Denise can try out for the role of the cowardly lion.
Ⓓ Boys and girls rarely agree on anything.

18. What is another way of saying "They proceeded to cast the play."

Ⓐ They began to assign character roles to people.
Ⓑ They began to practice presenting the play.
Ⓒ They threw out the idea of presenting the play.
Ⓓ They had a party for everyone in the play.

GO ON

Coast to Coast • Skills Assessment • Harcourt Brace School Publishers

COMPREHENSION: Summarize/Paraphrase (continued)

Colin will never forget the advice his dad gave him when he was a young man. Colin was getting ready to leave for college the fall after he had graduated from high school. He was a little nervous about leaving home and going out on his own. Although he had never gone to college himself, Colin's dad was a very wise man. He said, "Colin, you must always follow your dreams, for dreams are the most important things we have. They motivate us to keep going. They give us hope. Don't ever lose sight of your dreams, Colin." Colin still remembers these words although they were spoken to him many years ago. Colin followed his father's advice and, after graduating from college, he lived and worked overseas for a number of years.

19. Which of the following statements best summarizes this passage?

Ⓐ Colin graduated from high school many years ago.
Ⓑ Colin's father has not spoken to him in many years.
Ⓒ Colin remembered and followed his father's advice.
Ⓓ All of Colin's dreams came true because his father helped him.

20. What is another way of saying, "Always follow your dreams"?

Ⓐ Don't let your dreams get in your way.
Ⓑ Ideas will come to you in your sleep.
Ⓒ Try to achieve your goals in life.
Ⓓ Keep on daydreaming.

Coast to Coast • Skills Assessment • Harcourt Brace School Publishers

COMPREHENSION: Summarize/Paraphrase (continued)

> Darla was home with the flu. It was not where she wanted to be. She could picture her friends in school going to classes, eating lunch, and playing in the schoolyard. No one likes being ill, but Darla was trying to make the best of it. She read a book, worked on a crossword puzzle, and listened to the radio. She also drank lots of juice. The doctor had said she could go back to school after her temperature was normal for 24 hours. Darla knew she would feel better soon. In the meantime she just had to take care of herself.

21. Which of the following statements best summarizes this passage?

    Ⓐ Darla likes to read.
    Ⓑ Darla must drink lots of juice.
    Ⓒ Darla's doctor took her temperature.
    Ⓓ Darla is recovering from the flu.

22. What is another way of saying, "Darla was trying to make the best of it"?

    Ⓐ Darla was trying to enjoy what she could.
    Ⓑ Darla was doing a big project.
    Ⓒ Darla always wanted to be better than others.
    Ⓓ Darla could hardly wait to get better.

Coast to Coast • Skills Assessment • Harcourt Brace School Publishers

GO ON

COMPREHENSION: Summarize/Paraphrase (continued)

> Wendy awoke in the middle of the night, realizing that something was wrong. She glanced over at her clock. Two o'clock in the morning. What had waked her up? She smelled the smoke at the same instant she saw the flames outside her window. Wendy scrambled to the door but felt it carefully before she opened it, as she had been taught to do. The door was not hot, so Wendy knew it was safe to open it.
>
> By the time Wendy opened the front door, her mother was already outside drenching the flames with a garden hose, and her father was standing by with a shovel. They never discovered what caused the pile of dry leaves to burn, but they were all glad the fire had been detected and put out before any harm was done.

23. Which of the following statements best summarizes the passage?

　Ⓐ Wendy was injured in a fire.
　Ⓑ Wendy's parents put out a fire.
　Ⓒ Wendy was having a dream about a fire.
　Ⓓ Wendy's family figured out how the fire started.

24. What is another way of saying, "Her father was standing by with a shovel"?

　Ⓐ Her father was standing very close to a shovel.
　Ⓑ Her father took a shovel and walked away with it.
　Ⓒ Her father was digging a hole with a shovel.
　Ⓓ Her father was standing in a store where he went to buy a new shovel.

Coast to Coast • Skills Assessment • Harcourt Brace School Publishers

LANGUAGE ARTS

SKILLS	

Recognize Adverbs
Recognize Correct Comparisons with
    Adverbs
Recognize Negative Words
Recognize Prepositions, Objects of
    Prepositions, and Prepositional
    Phrases	

Criterion Score	15/20
Pupil Score	_____

Coast to Coast • Skills Assessment • Harcourt Brace School Publishers

Sample Multiple-Choice Questions:

The first kind of question is multiple choice. Carefully read the directions and the question. Then fill in the answer circle beside the choice you think is best. Question 1 has been answered for you. Look at it and then answer question 2.

Directions: Choose the **complete subject** of each sentence.

1. Tom ran to school.

   Ⓐ Tom
   Ⓑ ran

2. The cat slept on the chair.

   Ⓐ The cat
   Ⓑ slept on the chair

Sample Write-in-the-Answer Questions:

For the second kind of question, carefully read the directions and the question. Then write your answer on the line. Question 3 has been answered for you. Look at it and then answer question 4.

Directions: Write the **complete predicate** of each sentence.

3. We went to the ball game.

   went to the ball game _____

4. The game was exciting.

   _____

Coast to Coast • Skills Assessment • Harcourt Brace School Publishers

Directions: Choose the **adverb** in each sentence. Fill in the answer circle beside the one you choose.

1. Stay away from angrily snarling dogs and busy mothers.
   - Ⓐ stay
   - Ⓑ angrily
   - Ⓒ snarling

2. Theodore Roosevelt said, "Speak softly and carry a big stick."
   - Ⓐ softly
   - Ⓑ carry
   - Ⓒ big

Directions: Write the two **adverbs** in each sentence.

3. He had forty-two boxes, all carefully packed, with his name printed clearly on each.

   _____

4. The jury almost always took notes.

   _____

Directions: Decide what or who is being compared by the **adverb** in this sentence. Fill in the answer circle beside the one you choose.

5. Lynn's two young dogs play harder than Jeff's old one.
   - Ⓐ Lynn and Jeff
   - Ⓑ Lynn's two dogs
   - Ⓒ Lynn's dogs and Jeff's dog

Directions: Choose the correct form of the **adverb** to go in each blank. Fill in the answer circle beside the one you choose.

6. Chris clears the table _____ than his brother.
   - Ⓐ quickly
   - Ⓑ most quickly
   - Ⓒ more quickly

Coast to Coast • Skills Assessment • Harcourt Brace School Publishers

GO ON

7. Because of the lower gravity, astronauts can jump _____ on the moon than on Earth.
   - Ⓐ high
   - Ⓑ higher
   - Ⓒ highest

8. Of all the people I know, Nancy sprints _____.
   - Ⓐ well
   - Ⓑ best
   - Ⓒ good

Directions: Write the **negative** word or words in each sentence.

9. I never do my homework late at night.

   _____

10. He's not a very friendly dog, so nobody bothers him.

   _____

Directions: Rewrite this sentence to make it correct.

11. We don't have no money.

   _____

Directions: Rewrite this sentence to make it a **negative** statement.

12. This is Jenna's house.

   _____

Directions: Choose the **preposition** in each sentence. Fill in the answer circle beside the one you choose.

13. Go over the bridge and turn right.
   - Ⓐ Go
   - Ⓑ over
   - Ⓒ turn

14. Heavy rains arrived after the long dry spell.
   - Ⓐ heavy
   - Ⓑ after
   - Ⓒ long

Coast to Coast • Skills Assessment • Harcourt Brace School Publishers

GO ON   11

Directions: Choose the word in this sentence that is the **object of a preposition.** Fill in the answer circle beside the one you choose.

15. Alice and I walked slowly toward the city.
    Ⓐ Alice
    Ⓑ I
    Ⓒ city

Directions: Choose the words in this sentence that form a **prepositional phrase.** Fill in the answer circle beside the one you choose.

16. Inside the cage, green parakeets hopped and fluttered.
    Ⓐ Inside the cage
    Ⓑ green parakeets
    Ⓒ hopped and fluttered

Directions: Write the **preposition** in each sentence.

17. A little dog trotted by the old man's side.

_____

18. She came without a suitcase and didn't stay long.

_____

Directions: Write the **object of a preposition** in this sentence.

19. He received a letter from his friend.

_____

Directions: Write the words from this rhyme that form **a prepositional phrase.**

20. "I said it very loud and clear; I went and shouted in his ear."

_____

Coast to Coast • Skills Assessment • Harcourt Brace School Publishers

STOP!

Signatures

Coast to Coast

Skills Assessment

Roads to the West/Theme 6

HARCOURT
BRACE

ORLANDO ATLANTA AUSTIN BOSTON SAN FRANCISCO CHICAGO DALLAS NEW YORK
TORONTO LONDON

PART NO. 9997-17416-X

ISBN 0-15-308236-4 (PACKAGE OF 12)

5